HAVE YOU EVER WONDERED?

Geoff Wiles

sunshine press

Sunshine Press

www.eatingsunshine.com

First published 2014

Copyright © Geoff Wiles 2014

Cover by James Hickey

Print Publication Services by Connie M. Berg

Title: Have You Ever Wondered

ISBN: 978-0-9925421-0-8

DEDICATION

This book is dedicated to my loving wife Linda. She followed me to some very remote parts of Australia and overseas whilst I collected data for this book. Never once did she complain even though she was often left sitting for hours and travelled on some very rough roads that caused considerable pain to her neck and back. Without her support and inspiration this book would never have been completed.

Acknowledgment

The contents of this book were personally researched by the author. His thanks go out to the owners and staff of the establishments and organizations who allowed access so that the information could be obtained. Without this the accurate writing of this book would not have been possible.

The major portion of this book was researched in Australia but most of the contents relate equally in many other countries throughout the world. Some, although some are generic to Australia.

There are ninety four photographs included in this book. Many were taken or obtained by the author and thanks are given to the unknown photographers who also   contributed to the book. Thanks are also given to the South Australian Police Department, Great Southern Rail, the Ray Last Laboratories and the Forensic Science Department of South Australia for permission to use their photographs.

CHAPTERS

HAVE YOU EVER WONDERED?

HAVE YOU EVER WONDERED?

How a female changed the five hundred and twenty seven year male domination as a Beefeater in the Tower of London?

Moira Cameron was born in Furnace, small village in Argyll on the west coast of Scotland. As a child she spent most of her time, come rain or shine, and playing hide and seek, football and other outdoor games with the village kids.

If it was too dark or the weather was cold, her indoor pursuits were drawing and watching television.

Moira's childhood home at Upper Goatfield.
(House on left at bottom of hill.)

Little did she know she was going to make history and knock down the walls of the male dominated Yeoman Warders (Beefeaters) at England's landmark Tower of London.

The Tower of London is the most famous of all the medieval English castles. It dates back to the time of William the Conqueror in 1078. Its bloody history encompasses some of the most important events in English history. It is admired for its history and its architecture but remembered mostly for the bloody executions, torture and imprisonment of the prisoners who were brought there.

One King and three Queens of England were executed here along with many other notable people including the two young princes, Edward and Richard. It is said to be the most haunted castle in England with stories of ghosts frequenting the corridors in the dead of night. There are 20 different towers within the Tower of London and the eighteen acres of land that it sits upon would be some of the most valuable real estate in the world.

For five hundred and twenty seven years, Yeoman Warders have consisted only of men. They were formed in fourteen hundred and eighty five, by King Henry V11, the first monarch of the Tudor dynasty. A heraldic badge, the Tudor Rose, is still part of the badge worn by the Yeoman Warders today.

The name, Beefeater is thought to have come from the French work, buffetier. Buffetiers were the guards in the palaces of French kings and were assigned the duty of protecting the king's food. Another possibility is that it comes from the Warders' payment of rations, which included beef, along with mutton and veal. There are many possibilities, but the real reason is open for conjecture.

Moira lived the early part of her life in Scotland, attending school and then moving from apprenticeship to apprenticeship trying to find her calling in life.

At the age of twenty, encouraged by her brother and her mother, she enlisted into the army with a girl from the same village. Even though they joined on the same day Moira hardly ever crossed paths with her friend as they went their varying paths.

Moira spent three years in the Royal Signals as part of her trade but her brain was crying out for more stimulation. She transferred to the Royal Army Pay Corp and enjoyed postings to such places as Cyprus and visited Norway and Germany on various exercises.

After twenty two years, she finished her time at the home of the Army in Aldershot. In readiness for leaving, Moira had completed her training as a plumber and it looked as if this was where she was heading. She also had an interest in electronics.

In May, 2006, she read an article in 'Soldier Magazine' which focused on the life of a Beefeater at the Tower of London. Emblazoned across a photograph of a Beefeater was the wording; "Not just a job for the boys"

Up until this time no female had ever been accepted as a Beefeater although two other women had earlier been interviewed. The main qualification for the position is that the applicant must be a Warrant Officer in the armed forces with at least twenty two years of service. They must also hold the Long Service and Good Conduct medal.

She phoned the HR Manager and at the end of a half an hour conversation, arranged for the paperwork to be sent to her. It duly arrived, but it was two months later before she eventually returned it. It was to be a life changing decision and she had to be sure of.

In October, 2006, she received a phone call informing her that she had been selected to attend for an interview for the position. The interview was in November and she was the only female amongst six applicants.

Instantly a barrier was put up by some, and most thought that she had no chance of getting the position.

Moira had attended the Tower a few weeks before the interview and was being shown around by one of the Beefeaters. He went to introduce her to another of them, however, when the other Beefeater learnt that she was to be an applicant for the position, he refused to shake her hand. This really shook Moira, but worse was to come.

Approximately one week after the interviews Moira was told that she had the position but she had to keep it quiet until after Christmas. The powers that be wanted to be able to manage and control the media around such an announcement.

Unbeknown to Moira, somebody in the know leaked the information to the press. Nobody would ever put their hand up to leaking of the information, but Moira knows that they were paid five thousand pounds for the story.

Within two weeks Moira was being introduced to the press. They came from all over the world and Moira, dressed in her army uniform, stood looking down from the Waterloo Building as they all filed into the Tower.

In June, 2007, Moira retired from the Army to take up her new position. She had to quickly furnish the cottage within the Tower grounds and spent two solid days shopping. The only furnishings she owned prior to this were a television, a microwave and a bed.

On the 1st July, Moira commenced work as a Yeoman Warder at the Tower of London. At this point five hundred and twenty-seven years of male domination of the position was over. Another piece of British history had been created.

She wore a suit to start with. This was usually only for a couple of weeks but Mora did not go into uniform until sometime later as they wanted to make sure she knew the job. Moira worked at the Tower performing all the tasks for around six months before she commenced acting as a guide and taking groups around. She had learnt a lot from her male counterparts and commenced telling the story the way they did.

This did not go over very well and she soon adapted to telling it from the female perspective. This proved more successful.

Not all of her male counterparts were accepting of her and she suffered at the hands of one or two of them with bullying and harassment. The main complaint was that they were resentful of the attention being given to Moira when they did not receive it when they first arrived. This eventually led to two men losing their jobs along with their residences at the Tower. One of these men was reinstated as he apologised for his behaviour. The other then took the Tower to the tribunal and was offered an out of court settlement for wrongful dismissal.

This angered Moira, who in the first place had not wanted an investigation, and it was now all being made public and casting dispersions over her credibility. It was explained that wrongful dismissal didn't mean he was innocent, just that the procedures hadn't been carried out correctly.

Moira considers her job at the Tower not to be an arduous one for which she is very well paid. All of the Warders and their families are required to live on the premises and as such, small cottages are provided, at a reduced rental, along a rear wall of the establishment. Some of the living quarters date back to the 13th century. Moira likens it to residing in a small village within one of the largest cities in the world. The area in which she resides is called the Casemates, which means houses within the walls. All of the houses are different and very comfortable with all mod cons, everything is at her fingertips. Not everyone can say that they reside within the walls of a Royal Palace.

Moira's home, in the back alley of the Tower of London.

The day for a Yeoman Warder usually commences around 8.30 am when certain areas of the Tower are opened up and fire and health and safety checks are carried out. The Warders move from post to post during the day, usually spending about an hour at each. A normal day finishes at 5.45 pm.

In 2011 over 2.4 million visitors from all over the world visited the Tower of London and it is the job of the Yeoman Warders to show them around and answer any questions they might have.

A Yeoman Warder can almost be likened to being a Security Guard. They are required to do a certain amount of policing ensuring that visitors are respectful of the property and the people who work there. The ones who seem to come under the most fire from members of the public are the guards who perform ceremonial tasks at various buildings. They are not permitted to talk or smile and some visitors take delight in taunting them.

Normal police are not permitted to enter the confines of the Tower unless invited in. The worst case that Moira can remember in her time there was when a young school boy attempted to set fire to the inside of one of the buildings. He was taken from the premises and made to sit outside until the rest of his school group had finished. It appears he was put on the first plane back to his country by the teacher in charge of the group.

Many famous people visit the Tower and rubbing shoulders with them and showing them around is considered one of the perks of the job. Another, is that the Beefeaters have their own bar and social club. The bar is run by the Beefeaters and open all nights except Sunday. Many groups are invited to attend the club and are given a night tour of the Tower.

In all, there are now thirty seven Warders at the Tower. There is a hierarchical structure in place with the Chief Yeoman Warder being followed by the Yeoman Gaoler and then five Yeoman Sergeants who are each in charge of a team. Tom Clancy, the well known author, is an Honorary Warder due to his writings concerning the Warders. One interesting facet in life at the Tower is that one of the Beefeaters has the title of The Ravenmaster. It is his duty to each day purchase a quantity of meat from the butchers at the Smithfield Meat Market and feed it to the ravens that live at the Tower. There is a complement of six ravens at the Tower and all have been given names. Most of the Ravens are rescued birds from the wild or have been bred in captivity and come from either Dorset,

Wales or Scotland. These ravens have been residing at the Tower since the time of King Charles ll and legend maintains that should these ravens ever leave the Tower, the Tower and the Monarchy would crumble. The ravens are free to fly around the Tower area but their lifting feathers are trimmed by the Ravenmaster so that they cannot fly over the walls. What bird would want to leave such surroundings when all they have to do is line up for their meal every day? (Moira may become the first bird to feed the birds). One raven did however escape from the Tower and was found five days later at Greenwich by a vigilant member of the public.

As much as Moira loves her job she states that at times it can seem like being under house arrest and that on her days off she has to try and get away from the premises. She still spends some time sightseeing around London but likes to get away into the country visiting friends.

Her working time usually involves seven days on and then either two or three off before coming back for another seven. This roster works over a twenty eight day period.

Moira in uniform with the Tower of London in the background.

She loves the ceremonial uniform that she is required to wear and makes full use of its deep pockets for carrying around what she may need during a day. The only down side to it is that the uniform, especially the hat, can be very hot to wear on a warm day.

One memorable story that Moira remembers is back when she first commenced duties at the Tower and was approached by an American couple who were having their first holiday without their children. They told Moira that when their youngest daughter first read of Moira's appointment as a Yeoman Warder, she turned to them and said, "This means that I can now do anything in life." This story really touched Moira and it is one that she remembers with fondness.

It is true, one of the last male only bastions, has been infiltrated by a woman. From the comments being put about by the public, press and those in officialdom, it was about time.

The young girl from a small remote Scottish village could never have imagined the impact she would have on British history. Others will follow in her footsteps but she will always be the ground-breaker.

HAVE YOU EVER WONDERED?

WHAT IT WOULD BE LIKE TO BE A MEMBER OF A POLICE STAR GROUP.

As a model for this chapter we chose the elite South Australian Police Special Tasks and Rescue Group but most similar groups around the world can be related to what we discuss here.

The Special Task and Rescue (STAR) Operations Unit were first formed in 1978 and since that time more than two hundred and fifty two officers have passed through its ranks.

STAR Operations Unit is part of the STAR Group which has other units such as Water Operations Unit, Dog Operations Unit, Mounted Operations Unit, Explosive Co-ordination Section and Negotiation Co-ordination Section.

The STAR Operations Unit at the present time have fifty five trained officers in the group. The members are trained in all aspects of high risk policing. They all become proficient in dealing with armed and dangerous offenders, counter terrorism response, cliff rescue and rescue management.

When a member joins STAR Operations Unit they are given a numbered plaque which is erected on the Honour Roll of members that adorn the walls of the corridors of their building. When the member leaves they take the plaque with them and leave behind, in its place, a photo of themself, so that the memory is perpetuated in the history of the unit.

A course is usually conducted every 12 months with applicants for the course needing a minimum of two years police experience behind them. The course is a rigorous one involving a one day physical test followed by a four day course based on the SAS training regime. During this the applicants are put through a vigorous regime to see if they are capable of making good decisions whilst under extreme pressure. While there is a big emphasis placed on physical fitness, there is importance placed on leadership capabilities, confidence and demeanour that will get an officer to the end.

To reach the final stage, applicants are assessed on the following:

Decisiveness; Emotional Stability; Initiative Leadership Skills; Motor Coordination; Operational Tactics; Planning Ability; Self Discipline; Team Compatibility; Confidence & Demeanour; Physical Fitness; Written Communication Skills; Police Procedures, Practices and Law.

It can be seen from this that no stone is left unturned in finding the right officer for the job. At the present time there is no female representation in the group, however, the position is available to women. One female has previously been a member of the STAR Operations Unit but has since moved on to other sections within SAPOL.

Thirty two applicants commenced the last course with only five making it to the end.

Once in the Star Operation Unit members undertake five weeks of intensive weapons training and commence a twelve month probationary period. Weapons tactics and search and rescue training then begins in earnest. Some of the positions that a new recruit may be steered towards will involve,

Marksman and observer, air crew, explosives and VIP driving.

The group has its own highly trained bomb squad. This squad works closely with the army but is completely autonomous from them. They have the latest in equipment and are ready for any task involved in the possibility of explosives.

When on duty in high risk situations a member will carry twenty five to thirty kilograms of equipment and must be capable of doing this, in extreme temperatures and for extended periods of time.

If anyone has viewed members of this group in action on the television news broadcasts they will see that usually only part of the face is actually visible. On a hot day it would be likened to working in a cauldron. The everyday uniform consists of fire retardant overalls, vests, helmets, goggles, glove and boots.

FULLY KITTED OUT STAR GROUP OFFICERS

They can work very long shifts and the tiredness levels of each member are closely monitored for their wellbeing.

Members are paid according to their rank in the police along with an allowance for the Star Group. This is not unusual as most specialised areas within the police are paid an allowance depending on their situation.

Members like to remain as long as they can to utilize the skills they have acquired. There is much blood, sweat and tears shed to gain some of these skills. There are said to be one hundred plus, skills that they can become proficient in.

Promotions within the group can take them to the rank of Senior Sergeant but they must then leave if they wish to advance to the rank of Inspector and once the rank of Inspector is attained it is possible to return to the unit.

The group is centrally based at Netley which gives them easy access to the airport should they need to use the helicopter. The helicopter is becoming an almost daily part of policing which includes, but not limited to high speed pursuits and searching for offenders and missing persons. While the police do not own its own helicopter they lease one privately. A civilian pilot operates the chopper with Star Operations Unit members being trained as aircrew and able to operate the high imaging camera and also the rescue equipment.

The group is split into four teams who operate either on day shift or afternoon/night shift. Another team is on days off while the last attends training exercises and attends to any callouts.

The training regime continues throughout the year with some members attending training courses interstate or overseas to hone their skills. Between seven and twenty officers can be tasked to a job depending on what the situation requires.

On Friday and Saturday nights STAR members integrate with other police members to areas such as the city where there may be a larger volume of patrons enjoying the entertainment venues.

There is a fully equipped gymnasium at the group's head-quarters and all members make good use of this before, during or after their working day. Other training is carried out at the department's Echunga training base or elsewhere as required.

The unit also has their own indoor shooting range where members hone their skills. The amount of jobs attended where the use of firearms are a problem, is now averaging around two a week and with society as it is today this will most probably increase. Luckily, tasks where police have had to fire their weapons are around one every two years. If we were to relate this chapter to a country such as the United States with their almost non-existent gun laws jobs involving the use of firearms would certainly increase greatly. There is always the possibility of gunfire when attending jobs and there is the well documented case where a Star Operations Unit member was shot many times when serving a summons on a person which resulted in a siege for nearly two days.

A twenty metre climbing tower also enables members to hone their rope and climbing techniques.

The vehicles utilized by the group include four wheel drives, station wagons and the Bearcat, a heavily armoured vehicle that is built like a safe. On one occasion in the United States one of these vehicles was shot at two hundred times but was still drivable. Its heavy armour protects the driver and the passengers and has the capability of a battering ram at the front.

Many an incident has been readily brought to an end by the offender seeing this vehicle roll up to their doorstep. The vehicle was imported from the United States with a price tag of around four hundred thousand dollars. It has a 6.7 litre V8 turbo motor that despite its size and weight drives very well. It is also fitted out with cameras all around with the capability of transmitting live feed back to command headquarters.

The Bearcat, ready for action

Most police services in Australia, in fact throughout the world, have a similar group of men and women, equipped and trained to the highest standard that enables them to deal with life threatening or high risk circumstances. It is to them we look when trouble arises and it is the men and women in these specialised areas that are willing to put their lives on the line to protect us.

Members of the Star Operations Unit are called upon when situations arise which are determined to be a high risk incident, which may include life threatening situations.

In general, police personnel are required to combat extreme physical violence or diffuse a difficult situation; it is all in a day's work for these officers.

STAR Operations Unit members are a group of individuals drawn together into a team situation where the life of one can be in the hands of another. Whether it is in the field of international warfare or the war against crime in society there is no greater force than that of a well trained organization.

HAVE YOU EVER WONDERED?

WHAT HAPPENS WHEN THE FLYING DOCTOR IS CALLED OUT TO AN EMERGENCY?

The fisherman, a tourist from Japan, drew back the long rod before casting again into the ocean on the wild, west coast of South Australia. Unfortunately, as the large hook, holding a small piece of bait, flashed past his half turned head it snagged on his eyeball. The momentum of the cast tore the eyeball from its socket and carried it out into the ocean.

This is just one of the emergency situations that the Royal Flying Doctor Service attends on a regular basis. In the year ending, June, 2011, there were over seventy six thousand Royal Flying Doctor flights involving more than eighty thousand flight hours and covering more than twenty seven million kilometres. Throughout Australia they handle more than seven hundred and sixty three patients each day.

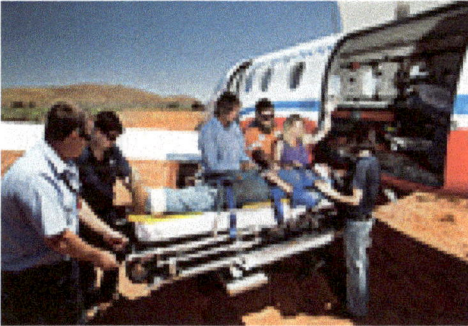

Each week, crews transfer patients to interstate hospitals, most often babies requiring specialist heart surgery or patients in need of urgent organ transplants. Organs going to recipients are also flown from state to state by the service. Attending at the scenes of road accidents many kilometres from civilization and flying the victims to hospitals up to a thousand kilometres away, forms part of their everyday workload. This can entail having the police cordon off section of a major highway so that the plane can land on the bitumen surface. There is not a lot of room when landing a plane of this size on a road and it requires exacting skills that the pilots have gathered in their years of flying.

There are no wind socks to help them gauge any cross winds that they may encounter and if carrying out this type of landing at night they have only the lights of vehicles positioned strategically to guide them in. The nearest landing strip may be more than one hundred kilometres away and when lives are hanging in the balance these types of risks have to be taken.

The above photo shows a remote road in the Pilbara   Region of north Western Australia where a vehicle had rolled over, killing two and injuring four others. The first Royal Flying Doctor plane landed on the roadway near the accident scene and a second plane landed shortly after a short distance away

Another is the plight of a teenage girl living in the Flinders Ranges, about 400 kilometres from Adelaide.

It was a very hot summer night in the Flinders Ranges town of Blinman and Rhianna, a typical country teenager was preparing to go to bed. She had just returned from a trip to Adelaide finalizing her upcoming course at the Adelaide University in Animal Science.

Her stepfather was the only person at home when she arrived. The house was in the process of being renovated and Rhianna planned to sleep in the lounge where the new air conditioner had just been installed. Her step father was going to sleep in the ATCO transportable hut across the yard outside.

At about 10.30 pm Rhianna lay down on the mattress in the middle of the lounge room floor. Being tired from her long trip back from Adelaide she fell into a deep sleep almost immediately.

About half an hour passed before she was woken from her sleep by a sharp, severe pain in her left upper thigh. She propelled herself out of bed and turned on the light. Clutching her leg she looked back at her bed but her eyes could not adjust properly and she saw nothing out the ordinary. She ran across the yard to where her stepfather was sleeping and told him that she had been bitten by something. The pain was excruciating as she grasped her leg, to afraid to look at the affected area. She was not making much sense and finally took her hands away to see four little holes in her leg and a small amount of blood around them.

The reality that she had been bitten by a snake finally penetrated.

Her stepfather took the cord from his dressing gown and wrapped it around the top of her leg near the groin as tight as he could.

Rhianna fell on the bed screaming and hysterical while her stepfather ran over to the main house. He was shocked to find a two metre King Brown snake lying full length on the mattress.

The King Brown can grow to up to three metres and inject up to 150 mg of venom with each bite compared to around 40 mg by a Tiger Snake

Realising the seriousness of the situation with the King Brown being one of the most venomous snakes in the world, he knew the Royal Flying Doctor needed to be called but did not know the number. He rang the local post mistress and she in turn rang the Royal Flying Doctor to request them to ring Rhianna's step-father. She then drove to the house to offer assistance.

The Doctor from the base at Port Augusta rang and spoke with Rhianna's stepfather to describe how to give emergency first aid while a plane was dispatched.

The RFD flight was en route from Adelaide to a routine job in the north of the state when they received the call. Being in close proximity to Port Augusta at the tip of Spencer Gulf, they immediately headed towards Hawker in the Flinders Ranges. Vickki, the flight nurse, was in contact with the Base Doctor and assured him that she would be able to handle the situation without having to divert to Port Augusta to pick him up.

Everybody realised that in this situation time was of the essence and that any delay in treating the patient could be fatal. Rob, the pilot was new to the Flying Doctor Service, and although he was very experienced he had never before landed at the Hawker airstrip.

The mountains surrounding the strip made night landing very tricky. The landing lights at the strip had to be   activated by Rob from the air before he could commence his descent.

A PC-Pilatus en route to an emergency.

Riahanna's stepfather placed a wide compression bandage, fashioned out of an old sheet, around Rhianna's left leg and left the dressing gown cord in place so that there would be no sudden rush of blood.

Rhianna was still screaming and about 15 minutes after the bite began vomiting violently. She was becoming weak indicating that the venom was beginning to paralyse her.

Rhianna was put into a car and driven towards Hawker, approximately 120 kilometres away. About half way there they were met by the ambulance that had been dispatched to meet them. As there was no suitable airstrip closer than Hawker, the Royal Flying Doctor plane headed there.

When the ambulance arrived at Hawker the plane was already on the makeshift airstrip. The Nurse from the plane had to stabilize Rhianna before they could place her in the plane. She replaced the bandaging and inserted two lines into her to control her pain. Rhianna's left side was virtually paralysed. She could barely move her neck to allow her to vomit.

Rhianna remembered the Flying Doctor nurse as being amazing, which helped her feel that everything was going to be okay.

During the forty five minute flight to Adelaide the nurse administered oxygen to Rhianna. She was unable to administer anti venom as it is not able to be stored on the plane.

Upon arriving at the airport the plane was met by the ambulance and the patient was transferred for the trip to hospital. The flight nurse contacted the emergency section at the Royal Adelaide Hospital to inform them of the treatment she had administered so that they would be ready when the ambulance arrived.

Rhianna could not remember landing but only being transferred to the ambulance at the Adelaide Airport and being rushed to the Royal Adelaide Hospital. By the time she reached the hospital she was deteriorating and can only remember the Doctors trying to keep her informed as they worked on her.

Rhianna's mother and best friend drove all the way to Adelaide and by the time they arrived Rhianna was in so much pain that she told them not to touch her.

Unbelievably she had been bitten twice by the snake in the same area which had turned black and was swollen. Rhianna was lucky in that the venom from this particular snake attacks the muscle and not the organs.

As the muscles were breaking down they were being excreted from her system through the kidneys.

In the crucial twenty-four hour period after the ant- venom was administered all they could do was wait to see if the kidneys could handle the excretion process.

Rhianna remained in hospital for three weeks and it took her another two months to regain her sense of smell and taste. The only residual effect remaining is a permanent hole about half a centimetre deep in her leg.

These cases highlight the valuable assistance given to people in the outback of Australia by the Royal Flying Doctor.

The Royal Flying Doctor Service exists to provide a high quality and comprehensive health care service to all people who live, work and travel in the isolated Australian outback. The operating bill for the Royal Flying Doctor is around thirty three million dollars nationally and the service has to raise a good portion of this from fund raising or private donations.

It is bewildering that an essential service such as this, cannot access more Government funding. Almost all of the services offered by the Royal Flying Doctor are free to the user. With over twenty seven million kilometres being flown each year by the fleet of sixty one aircraft, this service is instrumental in saving many lives.

The cost to the Royal Flying Doctor after the purchase of an aircraft is almost two million dollars to make it ready for use. The landing gear has to be modified to allow for the conditions encountered on various runways and around half the aircraft has to be removed, reinforcements added, and creating a cargo door wide enough to allow for easy loading and unloading of stretcher patients.

A custom built stretcher system with a hydraulic lifting device to raise and lower patients to and from the aircraft is also added. The cabin walls and floor are modified to provide hygienic surfaces and the floor is raised and levelled.

Purpose built cabinets and shelves are added to house the medical and monitoring equipment. Safety equipment for those on board is also installed. The aircraft is transformed into a space where life-saving surgical operations, intensive care and obstetrical procedures can take place whilst in flight.

Communications are very important to the treating of patients and an integrated communication panel is added to ensure that staff can make emergency satellite calls whilst in flight.

The days of the service having to rely entirely upon the high frequency radio system that was in place are gone and replaced with telephones, two way conferencing and satellite dishes.

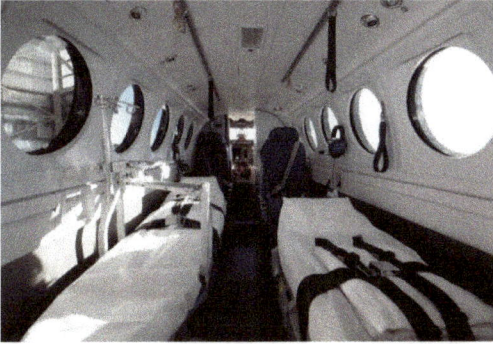

The inside of a Beechcraft aircraft after modifications have been carried out to make it suitable for Royal Flying Doctor use.

From landings at busy city airports to landings on rough remote cattle station air strips and even down the centre of outback roads, this service will continue to provide the medical assistance to those in need.

When the pilot and nurse commence each day they never know where they will end up as every day is different. The dangers of flying off to parts unknown are always present but they have a job to do. Without them, many a person would have died in the harsh Australian outback.

The Royal Flying Doctor Service covers around eighty percent of Australia, roughly the size of the United States, and some of it the most unforgiving and barren land on the earth.

HAVE YOU EVER WONDERED?

WHAT THE WORKING DAY OF A HEART

SURGEON IS LIKE?

Why is it done? How is it done? Who performs this work?

I joined an eminent heart surgeon who is the head of the Cardio Thoracic unit at a large city hospital for a normal days work. While only one hospital was visited the   following is a normal day for a heart surgeon, at most major hospitals throughout the world

A day usually starts around 7.30am when patients are seen during ward rounds at the various hospitals that he performs duties at. When these are completed he will then return to the main hospital for his day at the Cardiothoracic Unit. Patients to this unit come from   referrals from Cardiologists who may have been treating the patient for some time.

Surgery usually commences around 8.00am and on our day at the hospital a patient who had had a five-hour surgery less than a week ago was found to have blood pooling around his heart. He was going to have to be opened up again and the blood drained out. By the time we arrived the patient was already anaesthetized and the operating room staff was preparing him for surgery. The body was sterilized and then draped.

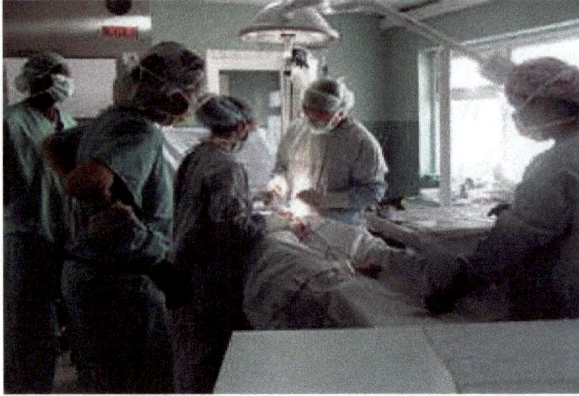

HEART SURGERY IN PROGRESS

Two Surgeons were present; one on either side of the body although only one was going to perform the procedure. The surgeons removed the staples that were holding the previous incision closed. This traversed up the centre of the body for approximately 30 cm. As the patients sternum had been wired together after the initial surgery these wires were now removed. Once all of the staples were out spreaders were inserted into the cavity to open it up.

Many sterile swabs and a suction hose were then used to remove the excess pooled blood from around the heart area.

This emergency treatment had forced another patient who was due to be operated on to be sent home. There is an acute shortage of after surgery beds available at most hospitals and this type of surgery requires patients to be monitored for varying lengths of time at the unit. We learnt later in the morning that the patient who was sent home had to be brought back to the hospital's emergency area by ambulance suffering from chest pains. This was not a good result but it highlights the lack of facilities at hospitals.

There was nine medical staff in the room at this time. Nurses had been busy prior to the operation getting under way counting out the instruments and swabs that were ready to be used in the procedure. This counting is done both before and just prior to the closing of the body so that everything is accounted for and nothing left in the body after closing.

The scrub nurse was in position alongside the surgeon ready to hand him whatever he required while the operation was in progress. The whole unit worked very cohesively with everybody knowing what was required of them in advance. There was no music blaring in the theatre as we are used to seeing on the television but plenty of friendly banter between the surgeon and the other staff present. In the real world people need to be able to talk amongst themselves and not have to shout.

When the surgeon was satisfied that all the excess blood had been removed he commenced to pour from a jug, a brown antiseptic liquid into the cavity. This is to make sure the complete working area is sterilised. This was later siphoned out. Plastic tubes were then inserted into the area to enable any further liquid to be drained out.

The sternum was then rewired by the surgeon and these wires will remain forever except in some exceptional circumstances when there might be some discomfort to the patient.

The final closing was left to the second surgeon present while our subject left the operating room to attend a meeting with other senior hospital staff. Unfortunately meetings of this nature force surgeons away from the operating environment for increasing lengths of time.

In the meantime the patient was removed back to the intensive care area and the nursing staff cleaned and sterilized the operating room for the next procedure.

Our surgeon returned to his office and dictated case notes for hospital staff to type for him.

With no chance for a lunch break the surgeon headed back to the operating area and scrubbed for the next operation which was going to require the patient going onto a bypass machine while a leaking valve was repaired. This time the operating room was staffed by 14 medical staff including nurses, by-pass technicians, anaesthetists and two surgeons. While the theatre was quite large by the time these fourteen persons were in position along with the various trays of instruments, the large bypass machine, various bins for the waste material and the anaethetheists machine it was almost to the stage of standing room only. In all there were seven computer monitors facing the various medical staff.

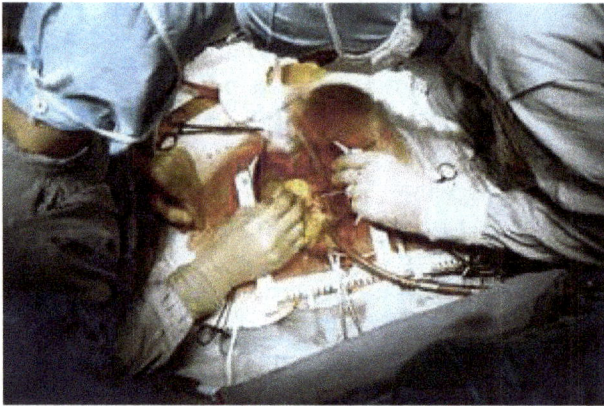

Bypass surgery in progress

The two surgeons prepared the patient by painting most of the visible body with an antiseptic solution and then wrapped the body tightly with a clear plastic sheet that was secured at the sides. This sheet is placed on the body for a more sterile environment and also gives the skin more rigidity and is cut through with the scalpel when the body is opened.

The surgeon then made a small incision in the patient's left side and a small camera was inserted through this and secured outside the body by a clamp that the surgeon had earlier placed into position. Just below this incision a larger incision was made and a hole approximately five by seven centimetres was opened allowing a view into the body cavity. The light on the already inserted camera lit the inside better than daylight. A monitor opposite the surgeon gave a view from the camera inside the body and another monitor gave a view from a camera mounted on the surgeon's glasses and giving the view that the surgeon actually was seeing. Because the patient was on bypass the heart was no longer beating and it along with some other organs were in a state of collapse leaving a gap of about ten centimetres between the organs and the rib cage. It was in this space that the surgeon was to work his miracles.

The surgeon worked for about an hour first cleaning the valve that was to be repaired and then making a device out of a series of loops out of gautex.

The surgeon worked with a skill that would make a seamstress blush with envy. When the valve repair work was completed a small amount of blood was then released back into the arteries to ascertain if the surgery was holding. When satisfied that all was well the patient was gradually taken off the bypass machine and everyone stood waiting for the heart to commence beating.

This took a while but eventually everything was found to be working fine and the closing procedure was commenced.

Once finished the surgeon left the theatre and the remaining staff went about the duties of putting everything away and preparing the theatre for the next surgery.

Even though his operating duties were now complete for the day and it was nearing mid afternoon his duties were far from over. It was back to the office to dictate some notes and then back into the unit to check on patients before rushing off to another meeting with hospital staff.

On most days the surgeon is lucky to leave the hospital before 6pm and more often than not it can be around 7.30 pm.

If we couple this with clinics held at country hospitals that require a lot of travelling your everyday heart surgeon certainly earns his money.

HAVE YOU EVER WONDERED?

How a young crocodile is transformed into an expensive handbag.

First there was the sound of crushing bone as the jaws of the giant crocodile clamped down, with over 3000 kilograms of pressure, on the swimmer's leg. Next a piercing scream of pain and terror followed by complete silence as the murky river waters settled once again as the swimmer was carried to the bottom in a death roll.

This is the story we often hear of crocodiles in the wild. Crocodile have reigned as the number one predator in the marine environments for millions of years. The present day crocodile differs very little from its prehistoric ancestors who stalked the earth, even before the dinosaurs. None of the known species of crocodilians have ever become extinct. This is due to their ability to adapt to the dramatic environmental changes that have occurred over the millennia.

The following is of the crocodile we do not hear about. The one that never knows freedom. We visited a crocodile farm in northern Australia and within the confines of the farm were almost 5000 crocodiles. The farm is set up primarily for the sale of skins but also provides a service to the National Parks and Wildlife Service in the relocation of problem crocodiles. There are farms that hold up to 60,000 crocodiles at any one time.

Crocodiles are reptiles and have scales and leathery skin. They rely upon the sun for warmth and energy. It is a little known fact that birds are actually the crocodiles nearest living relative.

The massive prehistoric creatures can grow to over 6 metres in length and exert a jaw pressure of 3000 kilograms per square inch compared to that of a human, whose jaw pressure is around 20 kilograms per square inch.

This is the story of the farm crocodile that has never known freedom and the wild outdoors but has been kept confined all of its life. Very much different from its counterpart in the wild who is protected by law and will live on for many years.

A young crocodile commences life usually during the period November to March when the mother lays her eggs in a mound. Now this can happen either in the wild or in a crocodile farm. In the wild the mother will gather vegetation from the surrounding area to cover the eggs while at a farm material such as hay and straw is provided for her. The typical number of eggs in a clutch can average around 50 with an egg measuring approximately 8cm in length by 5 cm wide. In the wild the temperature inside the mound remains around a constant 32 C for the 80 – 90 days of incubation. During this time the female crocodile will guard the nest even if it means not eating for the entire period. It is possible for them to survive for months without taking in any food. They are a one off creature in this world having the ability to hold their breath under water for up to three hours and to lower their heart rate down to three beats a minute.

When it is time, the young crocodiles begin to break loose of their shell by using an egg tooth situated at the end of their nose. Those having trouble will sometimes be assisted by their mother who will roll the egg around in her mouth to help crack it. Once these babies are hatched they are safe from human intervention because of laws drafted to protect the species. They are not however safe from other creatures and the mortality rate is very high. In the wild about only 1% of hatching survive to adulthood. Most hatchlings measure approximately 20-25 cm in length and weigh 60 – 90 grams.

However, while still in the egg there is the possibility they will be collected by authorized egg collectors and sold on to hatcheries and farms where they will be placed in an incubator for controlled hatching. A certain number of eggs can be collected each year from the wild for this purpose but this activity is strictly governed by the relevant authorities.

 The collection of these eggs is in itself a very hazardous vocation with the collector being lowered from a helicopter in a cage and placed over the nesting mound. The mother crocodile does not usually take kindly to this and will often attack the cage while the collector is inside trying to gather the eggs. Each egg must be individually marked on top and the egg must be always placed with the marking up otherwise the young   crocodile will not survive. Not a job for the faint hearted. There are stories of one particular collector   being lowered down without the protection of a cage and fighting off the mother crocodile with a stick, while collecting the eggs from her nest. An adult male crocodile's jaw pressure is approximately 150 times greater than that of a human.

A LARGE MALE CROCODILE IN HIS PEN

At a crocodile farm the process is much more refined with resident male crocodiles spending their lives in a large open air enclosure with breeding females in separate enclosures around his.

When the season is right each female is allowed into the male enclosure for approximately a week and the male will commence the mating process. Once he has serviced his harem he is back to lying around the pool basking in the sun until next season. Back in their own enclosures the females build their nests and lay the eggs. On some farms a billabong is used with male crocodiles living with many females. When the time is right the eggs will be collected by the farm workers and they will be placed in incubators alongside eggs that have been collected in the wild.

At this point it should be remembered that a saltwater crocodile can be described as the ultimate killing machine. The collection of the eggs is a very hazardous undertaking and there is one reported case of a farm worker having his head bitten off by a crocodile. When working around crocodiles one must never lose concentration of what they are doing.

The incubator temperature is controlled strictly at around 31.5 C and can be manipulated so that a higher percentage of males are hatched. This is preferable because a male crocodile will grow to a marketable length faster than a female. After all, this is a commercial enterprise and the less number of days a crocodile has to be fed, assists to make a better profit margin. Research has indicated that the cost of raising a crocodile in a farm situation is around $280.00.

A YOUNG CROCODILE NOT LONG AFTER HATCHING

Upon hatching the young crocodiles are placed in large temperature controlled indoor pens. The room temperature in these pens is maintained at about 28 C and the water temperature around 30 C. There can be hundreds of crocodiles in a pen and they are sorted according to size. They are fed every second day a finely minced mixture of chicken and kangaroo meat along with supplements.

FEEDING TIME AT THE CROC PEN

As they get bigger they are fed a coarser mixture of the same. The food usually will come from nearby poultry processing farms and allows them the chance to get rid of meat that is not right for human consumption.

As they grow they are moved to larger pens with smaller ones being left behind until they grow more. In the pens the more dominant ones will get more of the food and grow in size much faster than the weaker ones. These weaker ones eventually become the dominant ones as small crocs are added to their pens. As the young crocodiles grow they move through the chain of pens until they are eventually moved outside to individual pens.

DEATH ROW PENS

In a farm situation approximately 90% survive and this is because of careful farm management. Crocodile farms can expect regular visits from health and food inspectors with concerns for the animals well-being and also the conditions that any foods produced by the farm are manufactured.

Once in these individual pens they are fed and left for any scars that they may have picked up from their days of open living to heal. A skin that is completely free of scarring is worth a lot more than a scarred one.

At about 1.82 metres in length the croc is stunned with an electric stunner and then killed with a .22 bullet to the head. The bullet passes into the spinal cord bringing about instant death with no suffering.

The body is hung from a hook by its tail and sprayed with chlorate foam to sterilize it. After being washed clean it is hung in a freezer room with the temperature at 4 C.

It is then moved to a sanitizer and kept at 7 C until the skin is removed. This is a delicate process and takes about thirty minutes for each carcass. Care must be taken not to damage the skin. A crocodile is skinned so that the entire belly, throat and leg pattern are removed in one piece. The skin is then blasted with a jet of water to remove any excess flesh and dipped in an anti-bacterial solution. It is then drained and salted and then salted again 24 hours later before being rolled and stored in a chiller.

Overseas buyers will then visit the farm and pick out the skins that they require for further processing. These are shipped back to Europe where they will be turned into expensive Gucci or Hermme handbags and other items. A very expensive handbag can cost up to $32,000.00 and require the underbellies of two crocodiles

Crocodile skin hand bag.

The skin of the Australian salt water crocodile, Crocodylus porusus, is the most sought after skin in the world. Their bellies are usually devoid of osteoderms or   buttons. There are 22 species of crocodile in the world of which only two are endemic to Australia.

Some of the other products made from the skin of a crocodile are wallets, belts and shoes. The meat from the crocodile is available in many products such as sausages, pastrami, mince and the list goes on, from some supermarkets and specialty food stores.

HAVE YOU EVER WONDERED?

WHAT THE DAY IN THE LIFE OF A PRIVATE INVESTIGATOR MIGHT BRING?

The most famous and probably the first private investigation agency was Pinkerton's in the United States. While they still exist the methodology that they once used has now been greatly surpassed by modern   technology.

Firstly, we must look at what makes a Private Investigator. The number one requirement throughout most of the world is that they be licensed by the local authority. Gone are the days of opening and office and expecting the work to roll in. Everyone wants to make a dollar wherever they can and that includes the Government. In this modern age before you can be granted a license you are required to attend a course and be examined at the end on its contents. Once through the course, often Government run, there are the Criminal History checks to make sure that you are a suitable person. Once again, the Government puts out its hand for another share.

By the time you get through all of this, you have outlaid a considerable amount of money and now it is time to look at what equipment you may need. At the very least, you need a good digital video camera, a good digital SLR camera along with a mobile phone and a reliable vehicle. Later there come the concealed video cameras that allow you to take film right in front of your Subject without them knowing.

Now begins the task of getting some work. The majority of investigators start working for a larger company. As with most industries, everyone wants experienced agents on their books but some will try a newbie. If not content with working for someone else, you either can try to pick up some work yourself through placing an ad in the   Yellow Pages or on the internet but it is always hard to break into a field such as this.

Your work can be split into working for large insurance companies, government agencies or the run of the mill husband and wife type jobs.

A good investigator can usually find ample work in the insurance and legal sectors and this is where the main bulk of investigation work lies. There are not many good investigators that rely on private work to pay the bills. This is usually left to those on the bottom of the investigation ladder.   Who wants to work between 6 pm and 4 am when you can make a good living at this industry and still be home for tea each night?

Old ways give way to the new.

 A good investigator will become expert in understanding human behaviour, putting themselves in the best possible position to achieve the maximum result for their client.

Video surveillance is a specific discipline of investigations that requires the investigator to maintain a balance between many factors to be successful. The investigator conducting the surveillance can be compared to a tight rope walker performing a balancing act. On surveillance, they must balance between being "close enough" to the Subject to see everything and keep up while the Subject is on the move and maintaining a "far enough" distance away to remain anonymous and undetected.

Now to have a look at what a normal day may bring.

We could start with the day when I opened the paper to find that somebody that I had been hired to watch and obtain a photo of had been gunned down through his lounge room window. I had only supplied the photo to my client about 10 days earlier and no matter which way you looked at it, it should have been an open and shut case. Alas, a good alibi along with the distinct   possibility that a hit man had been hired from interstate and the case remains unsolved to this day.   Since that time I have steered clear of matrimonial work. We will however look at a more realistic normal day as the above do not occur very often.   But the possibility of something similar happening is always on your mind.   The unexpected should always be expected.

A day usually starts early, before 6 am when we arrive on location and take an opening video shot showing the time and date. A good surveillance video tells a story with a beginning, a middle and an end.

After the opening shot you must establish a surveillance position accounting for the various scenarios from a rural setting with various routes to the main roads to the urban setting with tall building and hundreds of people exiting multiple exits. Once you have established yourself in position you must sit and wait. This can be the hardest part of the job. You must maintain your focus, sometimes for hours, while waiting for the subject to move.

Now the middle of the story comes into play as you   follow your subject at a discreet distance wherever they may go. It might be simply to take the dog for a walk or a visit to the local shops or you could be on the move for a considerable time. You never know where you are going to end up doing surveillance and you must be prepared for almost everything. We follow on foot, buses, and taxi cabs or in cars. Exiting our own vehicles, parking them, hopping back in only to park again a short distance away. We do whatever it takes to get video of our   subjects, making sure that that the video footage obtained is steady and professional.

Finally the subject will arrive back where he started and this is usually the end of the story for that day. Of course there are the days when the subject does not move and you can spend up to 12-13 hours just sitting in your vehicle waiting. Try sitting in a vehicle for that amount of time without succumbing to the call of nature. "Wee bottles" and other devices are utilised by male investigators but it is not as simple for the females.

Before we get to the following the subject stage there are other factors that must be taken into account.

Meticulous planning back in the office to make sure you are going to the correct location and getting to know all that there is available to know about the subject. This can include details that you glean from social media sites such as Facebook or Linkedin. Internet sites, such as Google Earth can supply you with a photograph of the subject's home and you can check the surrounding streets for ease of access and parking. All the planning in the world will not help you if you are not able to maintain focus while on the job. It only takes a moment for a door to open and close and much can be learnt or lost it that time. Tenacity is another required attribute of the investigator. You must be tenacious day in and day out to constantly acquire video for your clients. There are a multitude of outside factors trying to prevent you acquiring great video- whether it is the heavy traffic, a nosy neighbour, the local traffic cop, a crowded   thoroughfare or a complete lack of anything but you and the subject. You must have a plan of attack as no two surveillance jobs are the same.

Our first job for the day is for a Government Department. They have asked us to observe activities at a certain address to ascertain if the male occupant who is receiving unemployment benefits from them has any form of employment. A Fraud Hotline call has indicated that he may be working full time without disclosing it to them. Arriving at about 4.30 am, we find two vehicles on the driveway and the home in darkness. A suitable position is adopted to observe any activity. At around 6 am a light comes on inside the home. Fifteen minutes later, our Subject is sighted when he walks out to one of the vehicles. As he drives away, he is followed from a discreet distance. At this time of the morning, there is not a lot of traffic around and we have to remain about 200 metres behind to lessen the chance of alerting him. After winding his way for about five kilometres, he pulls into an industrial area and eventually stops at a workshop. After parking his vehicle, he walks to the front door and opens it with keys he has with him. The roller door adjacent to the office area soon opens and our Subject wheels out a sign indicating that the workshop is open for business. He is in the business of spray painting, the same occupation where he lost his job at a car plant 9 months earlier.

We allow him to settle in for the day and sight another younger male arrives.

At about 9 am an approach is made on the pretext of getting some work done. Our Subject discusses our needs and hands over a business card with his and the business's names boldly displayed. From our conversation we learn that he has been in business for about 6 months and that the business is growing steadily. It is surprising what people will tell you about them if you sound interested and they believe that you are their next client. As we approached the workshop, a discreet video camera disguised as a mobile phone, was activated and we were able to gain some video of the Subject spraying a car panel before he walked over to us.

From years of experience with similar matters, it is no shock to us that this man is collecting welfare payments while at the same time making a good living at his new business. Some people get away with it for long periods but this man's free ride will be coming to an end very soon.

Upon informing our client of our findings, we are instructed to return around the end of the day to see how long he works. We take a few discreet photographs to go with our video evidence and leave the area.

The life of an investigator can be a lonely one as usually only one person carries out most jobs.

The next job is not until 12 noon when we have been instructed to observe a male person who we have previously watched attend a pre-arranged medical appointment. The appointment is at medical rooms just out of the city and we arrive early to get a good vantage spot. These appointments are to observe to see how a person presents in the proximity of the Doctor's rooms and compare it with their normal movements around the home. Some Subject's have been observed arriving at such appointments heavily relying on a walking stick and walking with great discomfort only to disregard the stick and suddenly lose their limp once they are out of sight of the rooms. These so-called miracles are seen a couple of times each year and do nothing for the persons claim. Others will get their spouses to drive them to the medical and when they leave they switch drivers once out of sight of the rooms.

Many a claim has been brought undone by alleging a driving disability and then being video carrying out this manoeuvre.

While most claims are settled before reaching the court stage I have seen others reach the day of going to court only to see the claim dropped when the investigator is sighted walking in with two or three video tapes under his arm. A person seeing this can never be sure of which of their activities have been captured on tape. It can be most embarrassing to start lying under oath in court and then have the evidence presented showing them to be lying. Many a claim has been rejected by the courts after seeing video evidence and many a claimant has had to foot the legal bills for both sides. There is the well-documented case of a female on a claim for a bad neck being observed at a secluded beach with a male person. She was videoed carrying out a sex act on the male person that required a good range of neck movement. When this case reached, court and she realised that she had been caught in a very compromising position she promptly withdrew her claim. There was no way she wanted the video to be shown in front of her husband.

Today we wait for our man to arrive half expecting him to put on a turn. On our previous observations of him, he has varied his presentation from showing no sign of a restriction to walking with a pronounced limp.

When he arrives and alights from his vehicle the video camera begins to roll. Alas, our Subject walks to the rooms with only a very slight limp. About half an hour later, he walks back to his vehicle still with the same slight limp. He is followed away from the medical   appointment with the hope that he may attend somewhere where he will present differently. The whole aim of the exercise is to try to show a difference in presentation around the medical rooms to elsewhere. Unfortunately, our man attends a shopping centre and presents with the same slight limp as before. Despite following him around the centre and obtaining video of him by using a video camera disguised as a mobile phone we can obtain no useful evidence that he may be fraudulent.

Not everyone investigated is fraudulent but companies must be shown to be diligent when claims are made. Quite often, there will be a degree of disability that will substantiate a claim being instigated. However, often there will be an exaggeration for the benefit of increasing a monetary payout. If these are not investigated properly then all other policyholder's or taxpayers will end up paying more out of their pockets.

When our man leaves the shopping centre, we follow him home just to ensure that nothing untoward might happen and then leave off. Sometimes with such medicals, we would look at the Subject the day before and the day after the medical just to see how he presents. Most people making claims are genuine but it is the few who would rort the system that we are always on the lookout for. Catching one of these can be quite satisfying. They make life difficult for the genuine person trying to make a claim.

It is now time to go back to our first job as the client wishes us to ascertain what time he closes the workshop. Arriving back there, we find his vehicle still present and the doors wide open. Finding a suitable position that allows us a view of the area we settle down for what sometimes will be a long wait. It is not possible to see into the workshop without arousing suspicion but our morning's video shows what he is doing.

At around 5.30 pm the front doors to the workshop are closed and the younger male leaves in his vehicle. Not long after this the Subject leaves locking the workshop door behind him. Just to be on the safe side we do not follow him home, as we do not wish to chance alerting him to our presence. As the client is closed by this time of the day we take it upon ourselves to return to the workshop early, the next morning to observe the   Claimant arrive and thus prove continuity at the workplace.

Most working days would end around this time but   tonight we have what the industry calls a "private job". That is one where we are working directly for a client, usually and husband or wife, to see what their partner is doing.

This female client has contacted us and informed us that she suspects her partner to be playing up on his usual weekly night out with the boys. We have been informed what time he usually leaves home, what he drives, a   description of him and where he is supposed to be   going. Most of this type of job turns out to paranoia on the part of the client but each case must be taken on its own merit and sometimes there are surprising results.

We arrive at 7.00 pm with the expected time of 7.30 pm for the client's partner to leave home. His vehicle is on the driveway. With only one exit from the street, we position away from the home so as not to alert him by following him from there.

At 7.50 pm, the Subject drives past our position and we follow him at a discreet distance. Twenty minutes later, he arrives at the hotel where he has told his wife he is going. He parks in the car park and walks into the front bar area. We enter a few minutes later and position at the opposite end of the bar. The Subject is with two other males drinking at the bar. After a couple of drinks, an eight ball table becomes free and they adjourn there for a few games. At 9.45 pm, the men are in the throes of winding up their evening and we adjourn to the car park to follow the Subject home. It has been like most other jobs of this type, quite uneventful.

The Subject leaves just after 10 pm and drives a short distance in the opposite direction to his home. He turns off the main road into a side street and brings his vehicle to a halt. Being unable to immediately stop without alerting him to our presence we continue past and stop just around the corner from him. Hurrying back on foot we see the Subject walk back to the main road and go from view. Hurrying back to where he was last sighted we find that he is gone from view. With nowhere to go except into one of the nearby houses, we return to our vehicle and position it on the road where he was last seen to see which of the houses he leaves.

One house immediately catches our attention because it has the house number painted boldly in big white letters on the brickwork of the house. From previous experience, this is a good indication that it may be a brothel as they often use this type of numbering to make sure their clients can find the right address. No brothel owner wants a client knocking on the neighbour's door instead. While a lot of neighbours to brothels have a fair idea what is going on next door, having it substantiated is not what a brothel owner wants.

Sure enough, our Subject emerges from this house about twenty minutes later and returns to his vehicle. We then follow him back to his address and he goes inside.

Having been instructed to contact the Client the next morning with our results we return to the house the   Subject had visited and make some pretext inquiries that reveal that there is an $80 charge for a full service at the establishment with other varying charges depending on what we may like done.

This is not the result that we enjoy passing on to our client. What she does from this point is up to her.

This brings to an end a rather long day. Thankfully, this is not the norm.

An investigator's life can be exciting but more often than not, it is the opposite. Never   knowing what is around the next corner or what the next job will bring can in itself be the excitement.

Obtaining a satisfying result, no matter which way it might be, is a reward that makes the job worth doing. Couple this with the ability to bring in very good money is the reason I have not yet fully retired from the business.

HAVE YOU EVER WONDERED?

WHAT HAPPENS IN A DAY ON THE WORLDS LARGEST CATTLE STATION?

I travelled to Anna Creek Station approximately eight hundred kilometres north of Adelaide. The station is owned by S Kidman & Co and comprises approximately twenty four thousand square kilometres or 6 million acres. The Kidman Empire spans seventeen stations covering over one hundred and ten thousand square kilometres.

Anna Creek station complex.

They have around two hundred thousand head of cattle at these properties with most of the meat being destined for markets in Japan, south-east Asia and the United States. At the present time there are just over eighteen thousand four hundred head of cattle at the Anna Creek station with more expected. Most of these cattle are shipped to abattoirs at Murray Bridge or Naracoorte. Because of this factor the viability of the station was not threatened by the recent live trade dispute.

The current season has produced much needed rain and food growth which has enabled the station to restock after the drought years. Unfortunately the restocking is regulated by the Government who dictate the number of cattle allowed depending on the location of the property and the amount of feed available. When the drought was at its worst there were less than one thousand head of cattle on the property. When the prolonged drought   finally ended in 2009 cattle were sourced from wherever they could get them. This sort of country is best suited to Santa Gertrudis cattle but a lot of Brahman cows were sourced from other stations. Santa bulls are now being put over the Brahman cows. The property itself is bigger than Israel and 8 times larger than the USA's largest cattle station, King Ranch, in Texas. It is divided up into approximately forty paddocks and watered by fifty   artesian bores and tanks.

Cattle being yarded.

There are ten cattle yards on Anna Creek with a further four at the outstation at Peake. At mustering time, which can stretch over a number of months, all of the cattle have to be put through the yards. The cattle are drafted according to their age, sex and condition.

The aim of the station manager, Norm Sims is to grow the steers, aiming for a dressed weight of 300 kilograms. Some of the cattle yards on the property are ninety to one hundred kilometres from the homestead and it is more economical to truck the stock to the homestead than to drive them in. The station has its own B double truck trailer combination which can bring around eighty eight cattle in at a time.

On the station is a private school house where students are taught by the School of the Air and a full time governess.

The current manager, Norm Sims and his wife Stephanie allowed us access to the property so that the day to day running of the station could be documented. They live on the property with the youngest of their four daughters. The older two now work in nearby towns and the other attends boarding school in Burra. Steph states that her four daughters have an outlook on life that city kids could not understand. Their lives have been shaped by the outback upbringing. While Norm is busy organising the workers and seeing to the cattle Steph looks after the payroll, pays the accounts, orders the food and other equipment needed for the station and communicating on a regular basis with the Kidman head office in Adelaide with a weekly telephone hook up with all the other Kidman properties. If she has any time left over from this she is either in the school room, the laundry or helping out on other station chores. Without her input the station would not run as effectively as it does today. Besides overseeing the station Norm is also the President of the William creek gymkhana. Along with Steph who is the Secretary, they often find themselves driving hundreds of kilometres to attend a neighbouring town gymkhana. These are important social events in the outback and it is quite often the only way staff at the station, get to meet the neighbours.

There is currently 15 staff employed at the station including a fulltime cook who prepares meals for 11 people three times a day. The main staple diet on serve in the kitchen is beef. The present day cook, Margie, has been at the station for the past five years but she spent the first twenty years of her life there before moving away with Gordon, her now husband, who was a stockman on the property. Margie's father and brother, Stuart managed the property for over 40 years. When Gordon was appointed head stockman in 2007, both he and Margie returned to the place that they both love and call home. They now live in the original homestead that was built in the 1860's.

The station is powered by its own generator that uses 4000 litres of diesel every month. Although the normal rainfall in the area is not great they have the ability to fatten the cattle at a rate equal to other stations in a more productive rainfall area. A great deal of the station's water comes from underground with sufficient pressure from the Great Artesian Basin not requiring them to do a lot of pumping.

Life at the station for the eight jackeroos and one jillaroo usually starts with an early rise of around six a.m. followed by a good breakfast in the homestead kitchen. Following this the work for the day is allotted either by Norm or Gordon and consists of either, working with the cattle, fencing, grading roads or other jobs around the property.

Depending on the job allotted to them workers can sometime expect a one and a half hours drive to reach some of the distant cattle yards. This drive is usually along a narrow dirt track cut through the scrub. Sometimes this work, because of its location on the vast station, can entail workers camping out overnight where their particular job is. Most of the cattle work is done utilizing motor bikes or quads with usually only the work nearer the homestead horses being used. Anna Creek was one of the first stations to utilise motor bikes and fixed wing aircraft for the cattle muster. It was not until the late 1970's that the station stopped using camels to pull the bun cart over the sand hills to reach the stock camps.

Drover at work.

Workers are paid at a daily rate and can sometimes work around fifty hours each week. Work on Saturday usually finishes around mid-day with Sunday as a day off. The lone jillaroo on the property, Sophie, grew up on another of the Kidman properties and loves the life. In her spare time she tends to her own horses that she has with her, preparing them for any gymkhanas that might be coming up. She says that the life enables her to save well as outside of the pub in William Creek there is not a lot else to spend her money on.

More and more females are looking to get into this industry with almost two thirds of the applications received by Kidmans coming from females.

The jackaroos and jillaroos all carry out the same duties and receive the same wage. While the girls may not be as strong as some of the boys, whenever they may find a task too much for them there are always willing hands to assist. That is the way of the Australian outback.

Some station owners prefer the gentler nature of the girls with the cattle and in particular their approach to the machinery and bikes.

Getting the right sort of person for the job is getting harder these days with the advent of the mining boom. Anna Creek has the large Prominent Hill copper and gold mine almost on its doorstep. Here, an unskilled worker can have a starting salary better than the head stockman at the station. Can you compare the quality of the working life between the two? I do not think so.

All staff live on the station, either in provided houses or the bunkhouse. They have their own recreational room where they can settle down to watch the satellite TV broadcast or have a game of eight ball.

Usually by the time they have finished their days work, cleaned up and had a meal they are not looking forward to having a late night. A relax before turning in for a good night's sleep before it starts all over again.

While a day's work under the harsh outback sun or in pouring rain can easily get to a young worker, not too many of them complain. They enjoy working in the   outdoors and the variety of their work keeps them happy. For any young person wishing to try this life there are openings available at various properties. Not everyone gets to work on the largest cattle station in the world but there are plenty of smaller stations on

the lookout for good workers. Being away from the tempta-
tions of city life can quickly enhance ones bank balance.

An unusual sight at Anna Creek is plenty of water flowing
though the station's many watercourses. Its times like this
that the worker's take to the horses in lieu of the motor bikes
to search out the cattle for yarding. The use of a spotter plane
or helicopter can point them in the right direction but the
ground still has to be covered. The workers on the station can
spend many hours in the   saddle on days like this. A defini-
tive love of the outdoor life is needed in a job such as this.

HAVE YOU EVER WONDERED?

WHAT IT MIGHT BE LIKE TO WORK UNDER-GROUND IN A MINE.

I travelled to Mount Isa in the Queensland outback where I spoke to Bill, a miner with over 32 years experience working underground at the Mount Isa mine. Bill spent most of his life working on level 19 at Mount Isa. When Bill was working, in the 1960's there were 21 levels with each level around 60 metres apart. Between each level there were other sub levels, 10 metres apart, that are the same size shaft but do not go out as far. This meant that Bill worked approximately eleven hundred and forty metres below the earth's surface with the deepest part of the mine still another one hundred and twenty metres below him. There are now another 13 levels below this or approximately another seven hundred and eighty metres deeper at the Mount Isa mine. Can you imagine spending all of your working life almost two kilometres from any sun light? All levels of the mine were serviced by one main lift that had a capacity of carrying two hundred and twenty men on two decks for lowering and lifting heavy machinery and equipment. This main lift would take about sixty seconds to travel from the bottom to the surface of the mine. There was also a small manual service lift that operated alongside the main lift. This one was only capable of carrying about thirty two men on each deck.

The old time miners working around the clock on eight hour shifts. In days gone by a miner's day began when he and his workmates are lowered into the bowels of the earth for their shift. When they reached their designated work level they stepped off of the lift and reported to the Crib room. This area is where they will eat their meals and gather at the end of the shift when the shift boss will do the firing of all explosive charges laid during the shift. It is the safest area of the mine with extra reinforcing. Every man had a tag that he must place on the out board when he commenced work and when he returned to the crib room at the end of his shift he had to move it to the in board. It is not until all tags are in position that the firing can be carried out. It is the only way that the shift boss knows that there are still not any men out in the mine when the charges are fired.

The day began when the four two man crews on each level leave the Crib room and go out in different directions. Their job was to lengthen each tunnel by drilling with their hand held drills into the rock surface. The rock face facing the miners would measure approximately five metres by five metres. The drill bit is eight feet long and they drill a series of holes into the rock face and place explosives in each hole. The explosives are connected to a central firing line that reaches back to the Crib room. At the end of each shift when all the miners are checked into the Crib room the shift boss would fire the explosives. The explosive mix used was a substance named ANFO, which in common terms was a mixture of ammonium nitrate and diesel. Each firing would lengthen the tunnels by approximately eight feet, so that in each twenty four hours the tunnels would gain about twenty four feet in length. Before each shifts crew could begin their drilling they were required to clean out the rock from the previous shift's firing. Miners were paid on contract, depending on how much they gained in tunnel length each shift. If there was a break down with the machinery and a shift could not complete their designated task so that their tunnel could be fired then the incoming shift would be required to finish the previous shifts work so that they were ready to fire. They could not then do anything for the rest of their shift and it would end up costing them money. The money was very good for the miners and having to finish off the duties of the previous crew and then not be able to dig for the rest of their shift was not very profitable. It not only affected the crew involved but the three crews working in that tunnel each day.

They would tunnel approximately 200 metres and remove all of the ore from this area. Once the tunnel reached this length they would fill it with wet fill and allow it to dry. When it was hard they would commence drilling a tunnel above the one they had just filled. This would go on, drilling tunnels in layers, until all of the ore had been taken out. On nineteen levels there were three electric trains, each with about 15 carriages, running around a huge haulage area about one and half kilometres long by quarter of a kilometre wide, like a huge football field. The trains would travel around the various shafts and were filled by ore that came down large chutes. The trains would deposit the ore into a chute which in turn took it to the crusher on the level below. Once it had been through the crusher it was loaded into large skips that were capable of holding 80 ton. These skips were sent to the surface via the main lift and emptied onto a conveyor belt and carried to another crusher. The men that worked in the mine, everyday, would, when they finished their shift come to the surface black. The level that Bill worked on was approximately two and half kilometres long by three quarters of a kilometre wide. They had a north end where lead was mined and at the south end copper was mined. In the middle was the crib room.

Working underground in the mine was a very hazardous job with an average of two men each year losing their lives. In one year seven miners were killed. These deaths occurred not through rock falls or explosives as you might think, but by miners falling down shafts and being hit by machinery. In one instance two men were conducting repairs on top of the auxiliary lift. For some unknown reason one of them had clipped his safety   harness to the side of the shaft instead of to the top of the lift. Unfortunately his harness hit the button that would signal the lift to move off. He would have immediately have realized this but was unable to unclip his harness from the side of the shaft and as the lift rose he was crushed between the side of the lift and the shaft. His mate stayed on the roof of the cage and was unhurt. Pieces of the killed worker were found right through the shaft and these had to be all collected and the lift repainted before anyone was allowed to use it. Other deaths had been caused when the drivers of the mucking machines have driven the entire machine over the edge of a shaft and have gone down shafts up to three hundred metres deep.

Vertical shafts, known as risers, connect the different levels of horizontal shafts and are serviced by ladders.

Mining companies collect ore samples from the surface to determine where the main ore body is and all of the shafts at the different levels are only travel ways to get to the large ore bodies. A normal ore body is approximately forty metres by forty metres by between three hundred to three hundred and fifty metres. When the miners reach the ore body they drill and blast it and remove the ore to large underground crushers before it is transported to the surface.

To gauge the difference between then and now I visited the Broken Hill mine where I spoke with Mick, a long hole operator from the Perilya mine. This mine is believed to be the oldest mine in Australia and has seen all the changes in the industry. In its heyday in the 1950's there were over six thousand five hundred men employed in the mines surrounding Broken Hill and since mining started in the town over 800 men have lost their lives in mining accidents. At the present time at the large Perilya mine there are around eight hundred employees.

A monument built on a hill overlooking Broken Hill's mining area and the town in tribute to the 800 men who have lost their lives while mining in the town. At far right you can see the spaces where each individual is recognised by a flower and an inscription of how and when they died.

Mick is presently employed in the mine that has a current depth of 26 levels or around 1400 metres below the earth's surface. The levels, or drives, in the mine are between seventy and one hundred metres apart with sub levels created between them. The present day miners still cover a full twenty four hour working day split into two twelve hour shifts. The roster gives them five twelve hour days followed by five days off. They then return to the mine for another five periods of twelve hours on the opposing shift. Some miners wishing to make some extra money will work on some of the days that they are rostered off.

On a day shift there can be between ninety to one hundred and twenty men working as compared to between seventy to ninety men of night shift.

Safety is the number one concern for the modern day miner with everybody being expected to follow stringent safety rules. To not follow the rules will mean a short working life at the mine as no rule breakers are tolerated. This helps too ensure that everybody that goes down the mine at the start of the shift returns to the surface at the end in one piece.

This mine has around five hundred kilometres of roadway below the surface and the men will either report to their work station by descending in the lift cage or by driving down the roadway. The majority use the cage as too many vehicles would be utilised in the confined roadways. It was not very long ago that there were   traffic lights operating on some of these underground roads but they have now been phased out.

As with all mining a shift comes to a halt with a firing of the charges laid during the shift. We saw that with the earlier era of mining all men had to be safely back in the crib room before the shift boss would detonate the charges.

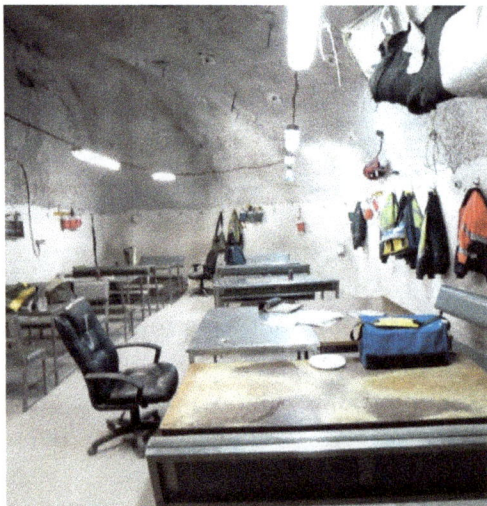

There are usually a couple of crib rooms, such as this, at different levels below surface where the miners can have their lunch break.

Being in a more safety conscious world the present day structure requires all men to be above the surface before the shift's firing is carried out. The Broken Hill mine is now firing at the end of every twelve hour shift instead of the usual twenty four hours. When a miner reports for work he uses an electronic tag to enter the mine site and will again use this as he goes underground. He also has a tag that he will place on a board before going down and must remove when he comes back to the surface. Before any firing is carried out all of the tags must be removed from the board to ensure all miners are above ground. This board is hallowed ground and any person found touching the tag of another miner will be instantly dismissed.

The days of the miner operating hand held tools and drills is now disappearing with the advent of machinery being utilized to carry out most tasks. Only in very small tight spots is machinery not utilized. The skills of the old time miners are fast disappearing. There are not many present day miners equipped with the knowledge and skill to operate hand held drills.

Dust is a crucial part of present day mining and all every effort if made to keep it to a minimum.

With modern technology having progressed so far in the past twenty five years it is hard to believe that the men working so far underground still only have the lights of their cap light and their machinery to operate by. Otherwise, everything is completely black with the exception of the crib rooms and the maintenance areas. Some of these maintenance bays are the size of a football field. The cost of providing copper wiring to the hundreds of kilometres of drives and work areas is prohibitive and so in that regard the modern day miner is not much better off than their predecessors. All of the power consumed at the mine comes from the power grid for the area. The only real advancement is the quality of the light now coming from the machine and cap lights.

Lighting is provided to the maintenance bays but to very few other places throughout the hundreds of kilometres of mine tunnels.

Gone are the days of contract labour with the modern day miner being paid a fixed rate, no matter how much advancement was made on the shift. A new scheme being trialled at the mine is where they are paid eighty five per cent of their wage with the other fifteen percent being paid as a bonus. This bonus is earnt by turning up for your shift, working safely, doing the job properly and the attitude towards the job and the fellow workers. It is a new system that has operated in other parts of the world but has yet to be proven here.

A 'new guy" in the mine can commence with a starting salary of around seventy thousand dollars which is not matched by too many others just starting out in a field. These 'new guys' can take up to three months to learn where all of the drives go once they get underground. A jumbo operator is usually the best paid in the mine with them being able to take home in excess of one hundred and fifty thousand per year. From all accounts, these men earn every cent of their wage and are the busiest men on a shift. They cannot have a slack day as the rest of the crew rely upon them.

Most miners in the modern era work along for much of their shift. They report for work well ahead of their rostered shift time and change from their civvies into work provided clothing including safety helmet and light and a personal breathing apparatus in case of trouble underground. There is a cage in operation and most miners descend to their working levels in this. Considering the length of the drives underground it can take some time to reach the spot where you will be working. Strict speed limits apply underground for obvious reasons. The drives are wide enough for two vehicles to pass but only with extreme care.

Driving through a mine tunnel on the way to a workstation. Electrical and communication cables follow the roof line.

When a shift begins the crews go in and bore a heading in a development drive that measures five metres by five metres by three and a half metres, much the same as the old timers used to do. All drilling is now done by machine and usually sixty two holes are drilled. A machine, named the jumbo is utilised in developing these drives and is capable of drilling out up to four metres of rock at any one time.

Machines such as the long hole rig are capable of drilling for 45 -50 metres into the rock with the machine capable of automatically changing the drills so as to be able to reach that far. The rock in the Broken Hill area is some of the hardest rock in the world and keeping a drill bit on course over that sort of distance requires great skill. These machines are used to drill out stopes, drain holes, service and probe holes.

A modern miner at work operating the drilling rig on right.

These are then packed with an explosive emulsion for firing at the end of the shift which is usually done at the termination of night shift when everybody working at the mine site is above ground. The next shift will then come in and water everything down to keep the dust settled and then the loader driver will come in and begin cleaning out the rock from the blasting. When he is finished there will not be a rock bigger than a tennis ball remaining. All of the rock is then transported either by chute or by truck to the crushers on levels twenty four and twenty five. The old time trains have been superseded by trucks capable of carrying up to sixty tons. Before reaching the crushers the rock is sorted by size and the very large sections broken up by a rock breaker.

The drives are then shotcreted with slurry of quick hardening cement spray and fibres to a depth of twenty five to fifty millimetres depending on the condition of the ground. Long bolts are then drilled into the rock to a depth of 2.4 metres through the shotcreted surface to further reinforce the drive walls and roof. This takes the place of the timber beams that the old timers would have erected throughout their shafts to prevent shafts collapsing.

One of the main tasks in mining is getting fresh air to all parts of the mine. To achieve this large fans measuring six metres by two metres attached to a large vent bag are used to push fresh air for over a kilometre through the drives.

Some of the machinery such as the loaders and the rock breaker are capable of being operated remotely from a control room on the surface. Here the operator sits back in a comfortable seat and while watching a screen in front of him is able to steer the loaders through the maze of drives and empty its load into either dump holes or stack bays. It is then taken by truck to the grizzly to begin the processing of the ore. The rock breaker can also be used remotely to break up any rocks that are too large to pass down the chute to the crushing area. Once the ore passes through the grizzly it travels down a chute to the lower depths of the mine to where the crushers are. All foreign objects such as metal bolts or rods are now removed automatically and the crushed ore is fed into large bins capable of taking around thirteen ton at a time to the surface in around two and a half minutes. It   empties from the bin onto a conveyer belt and is taken to the mill for processing before being shipped out by train for its destination.

In the not too distant future, it is also intended that the trucks and the long hole rigs can be operated remotely from the surface. This will mean the eventual phasing out of men and women below the surface and enable the mine to be in full operation for a full twenty four hours. At the present time the mine can lose up to four hours a day with the change-over of shift and the firing at the end of each shift when no one is allowed below the   surface.

The bottom level of the mine is occupied by a large pumping station through which all of the water used in the mine drains down to before being cleaned and pumped back up to the surface to be recycled.

Mining throughout the world employs over seven million people with statistics from the major mining countries showing almost fourteen thousand deaths. If we take into account the many deaths that may have   occurred in some of the third world mining countries this industry would have to rank as one of the most dangerous to work in. This does not take into the many thousands of deaths that occur after leaving the mining industry but that have been caused by it.

While mining may be a dangerous industry in which to work the advent of safer working   procedures and better equipment have made it a much safer environment for the workers. Their families no longer have to live with the fear that there is a good chance that their husband, wife, father, mother, sister or brother may not return at the end of their shift.

HAVE YOU EVER WONDERED?

ABOUT HOW A LARGE SHIP MANAGES TO

ARRIVE SAFELY INTO PORT.

Have you ever wondered about the relationship between the small tug boat weighing in around 400 ton and the larger cruise liner weighing around 150,000 ton or an even larger cargo ship weighing in excess of 350,000 tons.

How is such a small vessel able to control something so much bigger in size? First we must look at what constitutes a tug boat.

A tugboat (tug) is a boat that manoeuvres vessels by pushing or towing them. They are the unglamorous work horses of a port. They are broad in the beam, low slung and stubby, so that they have great strength in hauling and maximum stability in heavy seas. There are prominent rubbing strips all around and a high cabin with good visibility all around.

Tugs move vessels that either should not move themselves, such as ships in a crowded harbor or a narrow canal, or those that cannot move by themselves, such as barges, disabled ships, log rafts, or oil platforms. Tugboats are powerful for their size and strongly built, and some are ocean-going. Some tugboats serve as   icebreakers or salvage boats. Early tug-boats had steam engines, but today most have diesel engines. Many   tugboats have fire-fighting capabilities allowing them to assist in fire-fighting, especially in harbours.

How a small fish must look alongside a whale.

In March 1802 the first vessel designed or towing, the Charlotte Dudes, made her maiden voyage in the United States.

In the year 1817 the word "tug" was first used to describe these vessels and the name has remained.

Now, around 200 years on and the tug boat industry is still going strong around the various ports of the world. Without them, the large liners and super tankers and bulk carriers of the world, would not be able to sail. Without the tug boat they would not be able to dock themselves or navigate to places suitable for docking.

Working tug boats are employed throughout the world's ports to facilitate the berthing of such vessels. As the tourist boats become popular and the world's freight shipments grow so the tug boat industry will continue to grow proportionately.

Without this mosquito fleet the giants of the oceans would not be able to function. Some of these Goliaths of the sea travel at around thirty five knots and at that speed can take up to at least five kilometres to come to a standstill and have a turning circle of around 5 kilometres.

Even today when the latest ocean liners are able to   propel themselves sideways as well as fore and aft the tug boat is needed, even if it is only as a standby, in case the water currents or the wind conditions are not favourable. No port wants up to 350,000 ton of steel slamming uncontrolled into its wharf.

We will generalize when we talk about tug boats because they themselves can vary in size and power. In years past, the crew of a tug boat would have been between six to eight men. Now, on an average tug boat there will be a crew of three although some owners are trying to get the size of the crew reduced to two. With modern technology increasing the reliability of the boats they want to do away with the engineer. This will decrease their wage bill as engineers do not come cheap. The master, who steers and controls the boat, the engineer, whose job it is to keep the engines turning over and the deck hand that controls the working and mooring lines between the tug and the larger vessel. Some tug boats will be confined to river and near port work while others will sometimes spend many days at sea, depending on their location. In some parts of the world it is not unusual for a tug to be away from home port for up to thirty days. When this happens, spare a thought for the crew members who must work and live in close quarters with three or four other men where privacy is limited. The crew facilities on most tugs are very good and the galleys (kitchens) well equipped.

When a large vessel enters the restricted area of a port there is one more important person in the mix. He is the Pilot who is employed by the local port authority. He travels in the pilot boat, manned by a coxswain and an additional crew member, out to the larger ship and boards it before it enters the shipping channels leading into a port.

Sometimes a gang plank will be half lowered otherwise it is a long climb to the top from the small Pilot boat.

To do this he will climb a rope ladder from the small pilot boat up onto the deck of the larger vessel. This in itself can be a hazardous task as climbing a rope ladder in heaving seas is no easy task. He then proceeds to the bridge where because of his greater local knowledge he will control the ships movements in the restricted channels.

A Pilot, because of his superior local knowledge of the waters will know exactly where the deepest part of the channel is, how the tide is at a particular time, what can be expected of the local weather and how the currents may be expected to behave in certain areas. All Pilots are required to have a Master Class 1 Certificate of Competency with many of them having previously been the Captains of large ships.

The Pilot will position himself on the bridge and give instructions to the helmsman as to what course he is to steer and what speed the ship will travel at. When travelling in narrow channels constant instructions are being given by the Pilot.

The Master of the ship still remains in command of his ship but refers to the instructions and advice of the pilot. There is only one place in the world that the captain surrenders control of his vessel and that is when travelling in the Panama Canal. In almost every port in the world a Pilot is required to be on board. In those where it is not a legal requirement port authorities throw the onus on the ship's owners for any damage that may be caused. This usually persuades the owners to utilise the service of the Pilot so that they may be covered by the port's insurance policies. The cost cutting in not utilising a Pilot can have very severe repercussions if something should go wrong. Fortunately, these ports are few and far between.

Tug boats will arrive sometime after the Pilot has boarded a ship. Quite often only one tug boat is required but more are used as circumstances direct. The Pilot is the person in charge of the whole operation and the tug boat captain takes his instructions from the Pilot as to where he is needed and how the tug is to perform.

QUEEN MARY 2 ARRIVING IN PORT

On such large boats as the Queen Mary 2 where the ship has fore and aft thrusters to facilitate sideways movement the tug boat might only be there on standby. Some large ships such as the Queen Mary 2 are able to turn themselves in a full circle virtually within the space of their own length and have great control of themselves. Even with this capacity if there is a fast running tide or high winds they will require help docking.

The Pilot will instruct the tug boat captain where he wants the tug positioned and it will be done. The tug's deck hand will be on the foredeck ready to receive a thin weighted rope from the deck hands of the larger ship. Once he has this he will attach it to one of the thick lines leading from the tug's winch and it will be pulled up to the ship's deck and attached to a strong bollard.

The tug boat is now able to pull the larger vessel out from the wharf or control its movements towards the wharf under its own power. If the larger vessel does not have the capacity for sideways movements then the tug will gently place its very much padded bow against the side of the ship and push it into position. By being connected with the aforementioned heavy line the ship is controlled entirely by the tug boat. Often there will be a tug boat at the fore and aft ends of the ship to ensure a steady berthing to avoid any damage to both wharf and ship.

In ideal conditions one tug placed in the centre of the ships length would be sufficient for the safe manoeuvre.

Once the tug has manoeuvred the ship into position it will hold it there while the ship's deckhands and the wharf workers are able to secure lines in place to hold it in position. Only then will the Pilot instruct the tug boat master that he is no longer required. The winch on the tug will bring in the lines once they have been released from above and the deck hand will coil them on the tug's deck for later use.

The crew of a tug boat holds much prized positions with not a great turnover of staff. The ability to have an enjoyable working life, fulfil ones love of the sea and work from your home port is a big attraction to anyone seeking a working life on the water. The comradeship between men in the industry and also their standing in their communities has always been very high. Couple this with the fact that there is good money to be made and you can see why the turnover of staff is not great.

Unfortunately, the industry is undergoing change. Ship owners are trying all ways to cut costs and a present trend, spreading worldwide, is to cut the crew down to two persons and do away with the engineer's position. Their way of thinking is that modern tug boats are more reliable and there is no real need to have an engineer on board with many of his functions capable of being handled by the captain from the bridge.

There is also a 'dumb downing" of qualifications required to work on a tug boat. Once upon a time the captain of a tug boat was required to be a Master Mariner with years of sea going experience behind him. Now, a person can graduate from the Maritime College with his certificate in hand and be able to captain a tug boat. They have little or no sea experience and would not know how to splice a rope to save their life. Ship owners, in their cost cutting, are willing to sacrifice experience to save them money. One day it will return to haunt them as disaster is always waiting just around the corner.

The old skills of being able to work with ropes and carry out ship board repairs are fast disappearing. Regulations are now so tight that even if a crew were to replace an eye on a wire they have to send it ashore for testing and tagging before it can return and be used. It is cheaper just to replace the wire. Once the present generation of tug boat crews go most of their seamanship skills will go with them.

Tug boat crews are regularly drilled in aspects of fire-fighting and rescue, both of people in the sea and the rescue of boats in distress. Most modern day tug boats are equipped with fire-fighting equipment with high pressure nozzles fitted near the top of their masts capable of blasting water over a distance of 100 metres. The pressure exerted by the hoses requires the tug to be always engaged in a forward motion otherwise the tug will be forced backwards.

It is a little known fact, that when tankers berth they are required to hang a fire wire from the boat. This is because if the tanker catches fire, while berthed, a tug boat is required to approach it at close quarters and   connect to the fire wire and tow the tanker out to sea. While it is not a scenario that happens often throughout the world there is always the chance and the tug crew are putting themselves in great danger when doing this.

There is never any acknowledgement even though tugs move millions and millions of tons of cargo around the countries ports and contribute greatly to the nation's overall wealth. There is an old adage that when the tugs do not move nothing happens. They have been used as the front line in industrial disputes and their job has been crucial to bring about change in both industrial disputes and the political system.

There have been cases where foreign ships have arrived in our ports and the crews have complained about the onboard living conditions or that they have not been paid by the ship's owners for some time. `Here the tugs have been used as leverage, as the foreign vessel cannot leave the wharf without their aid, and disputes have been able to be brought to a satisfactory conclusion.

As with all jobs everything is not always rosy. The weather conditions can at times be atrocious and you do not have the liberty of saying, 'we will do it tomorrow'. The Pilot will have the final say in whether the weather is too dangerous for a ship to be brought into berth and if this is the case then the ship will have to anchor or drift at sea while waiting for calmer conditions.

Try manoeuvring a tug boat alongside a large ship when you are being battered by huge waves and belting incessant rain. This can quite often be the case and in some ports of the world, more often than not.

HAVE YOU EVER WONDERED?

HOW YOU DONTATE YOUR BODY TO SCIENCE UPON YOUR DEATH AND WHAT HAPPENS TO IT?

Varying regulations around the world relate to you donating your body to science when you die. In countries that allow this, the regulations will differ but the process will be similar. Instead of trying to cover all facets of the legal requirements, we will deal with the process in South Australia where they are to the forefront in this field.

Gone are the days when one could sign up to donate his body to science in the hope of getting an instant monetary reward. In the very distant past many a bottle of amber fluid was consumed with the proceeds of donating one's body.

In South Australia, the Transplantation and Anatomy Act allows members of the public to unconditionally donate their body for use in teaching, training, scientific studies and research in any licensed institution in the Commonwealth. The University of Adelaide, through the School of Medical Science, operates a mortuary for the acceptance of bodies donated for science and controls the transfer of anatomical resources to other institutions throughout the Commonwealth.

Donating your body to science is one of the greatest gifts that a person can make for the benefit of others by making possible research and training for our future medical professionals.

If you decide you wish to donate your body after your death, it is important that you advise your family of your wishes and ensure they agree with what you are doing. You then need to register your intention with the appropriate body in the area in which you live. The information with which you are supplied should be read and understood by yourself and your family members or executor of your will.

Regulations covering the donation of bodies may vary slightly depending on your location so we can only give a generalisation of what is required.

A Body Donation Consent Form must be signed by two witnesses and one copy forwarded to the institution where the donation is being made and the other retained by your next of kin or executor of your will.

There are two types of Body Donations.

 The first is where the body is donated unconditionally to the institution to be used in teaching, training, research and scientific studies. When they are no longer required, the   institution at their expense will cremate them.

The second type of body donation requires the institution to release the body when it is no longer required back to the next of kin or executor for private cremation or burial depending on their wishes.

Just because you have carried out all of the above does not necessarily mean that your body will be accepted. Some of the things that may preclude your body being accepted include the following;

1.   The donor has been dead for more than three days or cannot be delivered within three days to the institution;
2.   The body has been significantly altered by certain medical procedures;
3.   An autopsy has been carried out;
4.   Has undergone whole organ donation;
5.   Has certain communicable diseases or is suspected of possibly having certain communicable diseases;
6.   Has jaundice;
7.   Died with 24 hours of a surgical procedure or discharge from a hospital;
8.   Is obese or emancipated.

While acceptance of the body cannot be guaranteed, over 85% are.

If the body is not accepted then the next of kin will be immediately notified so that normal funeral arrangements can be made.

When it is accepted, a donation is final and will not be revoked.

Once a body is accepted it will either be embalmed that will preserve the tissue in a sterile condition or be sealed in a plastic bag and immediately frozen. It is then placed in either a secure refrigerated facility or a secure freezer facility until required.

The study of an embalmed body may continue over many years for continuous use in training the doctors of the future or for scientific studies or research.

In South Australia, an old and tried method of embalming is practiced.

A small incision is made in the neck and the carotid artery is raised. Another small incision is made into the artery and a tube inserted. This small tube connects to a larger tube that in turn enters a 20-litre container of embalming fluid. The container is raised to ceiling height and the entry of the em-balming fluid gravity feeds into the body. A tap inserted in the line controls it. Between 20 –40 litres of embalming fluid feeds into the body over the next 24-36 hours causing the body to swell up. The embalming fluid must reach every point of the body to prevent any bacteria surviving. During this time, the external body is washed 3 times with contain-ment fluid and the head is shaved. When all of the fluid is in place, the body is placed into a zippered body bag with one end left open. It is then placed into a refrigerator at between 2-4 degrees. Over a period of 3 months, all of the body's fluids will drain out and only the preservative fluids will remain. With the loss of the fluid, the body will collapse back to its normal state. The embalming fluid will kill almost all known diseases.

The body that is not embalmed but frozen will generally be used over a shorter period for the same reasons. Selected parts may also be kept indefinitely to assist in scientific studies, training and research. Frozen bodies are kept at -22 degrees and with controlled thawing, can be refrozen 3-4 times.

It is important that it be realised from the outset that the body will be utilised as completely as possible. Parts will be removed from it and turned into numbered or anonymous teaching specimens. Some parts will never be released, either because they will be required indefinitely or because of any possible risk to staff or students or will be disposed of through a registered waste disposal company. Once in the system a whole body can never be released. Only the remains, when no longer required.

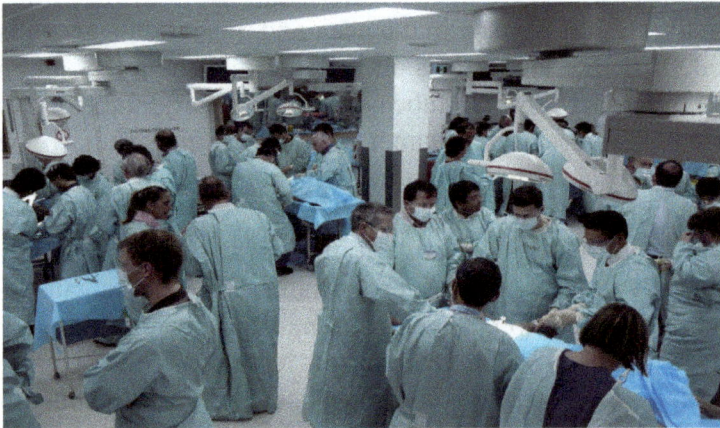

Medical students and doctors learn much from being able to spend time in learning facilities such as the world class Ray Last Laboratories in South Australia.

Sections of the body will be dissected to display muscles, ligaments, nerves and vessels that will be numbered and placed in clear museum pots to be used in teaching over many years.

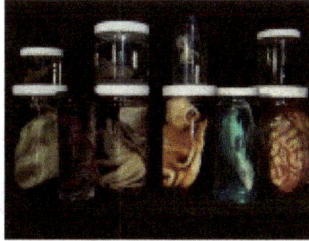

Others, such as individual bones, organs or muscles are removed for research into certain conditions or diseases to better understand the anatomy of a specific region.

Body fluids, bone, blood and fat removed during routine dissection, surgical training or the demonstration of new and innovative surgical procedures are usually disposed of.

The retention of some parts of the body is critical that the wishes of the donor, that their body be used as fully as possible to further advance science.

Although, all parts of the body are numbered and logged in a register, there will always be cases where to deterioration or extensive use they will no longer be able to be identified. These remains will be always disposed of as biological waste and never mixed with identifiable remains.

When the remains are no longer required they will be named and placed in a coffin. The Health Department will be then notified and they will inspect the remains and sign the appropriate registers before the remains are released.

For Type 1 donations, the next of kin will be notified after the cremation has taken place.

For Type 2 donations, the next of kin will be notified so that they can oversee the funeral arrangements with a Funeral director of their choice.

No matter the category of donation, a guarantee of the timeframe for a release of the remains cannot be given. It should be understood, that with Category 1 donations, there is the possibility that the remains will never be released, but in the majority of cases it will occur within 5 years. With Type 2 donations, a 2-3 year timeframe for the release of the remains is more common.

The donating of a body to be used in the advancement of medical training and science should be done for the right reasons and not because of the costs involved in the normal burial and cremation processes.

All bodies are treated with the utmost respect from the time that they are received and this message is conveyed to all students and researchers who will encounter them.

HAVE YOU EVER WONDERED?

HOW A BOTTLE OF BEER IS MANUFACTURED?

Have you ever wondered what goes into the process before you can place the bottle to your lips?

Over 1.5 billion hectolitres of beer is consumed around the world each year; the majority of this is contained in glass bottles.

The oldest proven records of beer being manufactured go back 6000 years with China now being the world's greatest manufacturer.

Beer is defined as being an alcoholic beverage made by the brewing and fermentation of cereals, such as malted barley, yeast and water. Adding hops to preserve against infection and add the bitter taste came from the French.

The process commences at the glass factory where fine sand, shell grit, soda ash and feldspar are mixed together in large silos and then melted down into a liquid by one thousand degree Celsius heat. This process takes place in a large shed commonly called, "The Batch House". The process can take around one and a half days from when the sand mix is added to the furnace until it is ready to come out.

As the heat turns these products into liquid crushed recycled glass is fed into the system and eventually the complete mix is molten glass. Depending on the colour of the soon to be completed product chemicals such as chromite, cobalt and carbon dust are also added.

The liquidizing process begins.

The molten glass is then conveyed via a series of tubes to an area where moulds are used to shape the bottles. The whole process is automated with the production line being kept moving twenty four hours a day, every day of the year.

Bottles coming in as liquid glass and being moulded into the finished product.

After the bottle is formed random bottles are picked from the production line and weighed. Strict guidelines must be adhered to as every bottle must be exactly the same as the rest. The weight of the bottle determines the interior volume. Where any discrepancies are found they must be immediately rectified. As the production line cannot be halted all bottles produced from the time the fault is located until it is rectified must be discarded. These are automatically removed from the line and sent to a crusher to be crushed and join the process again at a later date.

Once a bottle is made it still has to go through a series of checks so that absolutely no faulty bottles leave the   factory. One of these checks concerns the mouth of the   bottle where the cap is to be later fitted.

Once all checks have been carried out the bottles are ready to be automatically loaded onto wooden pallets and then shrink wrapped for their eventually shipment to a buyer's premises.

From the time a grain of sand is fed into the furnace at the start of the procedure it can take between one and two days before that same grain makes it onto the pallet, ready for shipment, albeit, in a different form.

The glass manufacturer that we visited, Amcor, in South Australia produces around 1.8 million bottles everyday and on a world scale they are but a minnow.

Large semi-trailer loads of pallets of bottles leave the factory every day. Some are loaded by fork lift and others by a roll on roll off method that is fully automatic.

Once unloaded at the brewery the bottles again join another production line where they are filled with beer.

To view this process I visited Coopers Brewery in South Australia where three quarters of a million bottles of beer are processed each day on a two shift roster.

This brewery like many others throughout the world has its own generation plant powered by gas turbines and draws its water from underground. This water is brackish when it reaches the surface. After treatment by a reverse osmosis process ninety per cent is usable.

Beer is defined as an alcoholic beverage made by brewing cereals, such as barley, with yeast and water. To add flavour, hops are also added.

There are two main types of beer production: the old British method using yeast which forms a cap on the fermenting liquid and produces ale, and the European method in which different yeast types ferment within the liquid and produce lager.

Ale is made in open vats and the yeast cap skimmed off near the end of fermentation before the ale is filled into barrels or bottled. Lager is fermented in closed tanks until finished, then filtered and pumped to laagering tanks where it is stored at cool temperatures to mature. Lager comes from the German word for store, or rest.

Within these classes, the difference in the making of the different beers is the amount of each ingredient and the time allowed for fermentation. The water going into the mix has to be purified and the barley has to be screened for imperfections.

Before coming to the brewery, barley must be malted, a process which converts the starch in the grains to the sugar maltose. This is carried out by first soaking the barley for several days them draining and spreading it over a clean floor in the malt house to a depth of eight inches at a temperature of 60 degrees F.   The process takes 8-15 days, during which is turned every 12-24 hours and sprayed lightly with water.

As the grains germinate the shoot or spire increases in length until, when it is the same as the grain, all starch has become maltose. It is then dried and kilned, first to slowly dry it at 100 F, then at 170-220 F to cure it. After this, it is rumbled to remove the dried spires and is then ready for mashing.

The barley is filtered in through a series of pipes with water being added to release the sugars. Then the mix is mashed in a giant pot to break down the starches and ferment the mix. The mix is then re circulated through filters and water added. This is called sparging and all the remaining sugars are removed. It is boiled for about ninety minutes in a giant kettle type   container with a double bottom and steam circulated though it hops being added to it to provide the bitter taste. The mixture is then drained to separate the liquid and the solids before being cooled down. At this point yeast is added and the brew allowed to ferment. Depending on the type of beer flavours are now added.

This process is fully automatic and is overseen by an operator in the brewer house. It is a very delicate operation with the liquid changing containers several times. All care is taken as the brewery has to be able to guarantee no contamination of its product.

With around two hundred and fifty six thousand litres of beer per day leaving the brewery it is not hard to see what one of the most popular beverages is. All this beer is transported away by truck and delivered to outlets throughout Australia and beyond.

Water plays in important part in the mashing stage. In regions where it is alkaline, the flavour of the malt is accentuated, so that the finished beers have stronger malt flavour and need fewer hops. These make many of the German beers.

If the local water is almost pure and soft, the beers made have more delicate malt character and distinctive pure hop flavour and aroma. These are the pilseners.

Certain waters in Britain have gypsum content which creates a notable character in ales and gave rise to the famous Burton ales.

HAVE YOU EVER WONDERED?

HOW AND WHY A SNAKE FARM OPERATES AND WHAT GOES ON THERE.

Zisiqiao is renowned as China's premier centre of snake farming. The locals have been raising snakes since the 1980s. Currently, about 800 people in Zisiqiao work in snake farming industry, raising some 3 million snakes a year. Live snakes are supplied to specialty restaurants; dried or preserved in alcohol and are sold to manufacturers of traditional Chinese medicines. Snake-infused wine is made as well.

On a lesser scale I visited the premises of Venom Supplies in the Barossa Valley in South Australia. They have a total of 600 snakes on their property and the main aim of the business is the sale of snake venom. Included in this number are snakes from 12 exotic species and 36 Australian species. The majority of their venom goes to research laboratories where scientists study the venom to try and ascertain how and why it works. The main product produced by them is used as a human therapeutic to stop bleeding during surgery. It is a post coagulant and initiates clotting of the human blood.

Venom Supplies raise most of their snake stocks on the property with very little being sourced from the wild. They have permits to take snakes from the wild if they wish but find that snakes bred in captivity are easier to handle and there is less chance of disease being introduced to their stock.

The majority of their snakes are native to Australia but some exotic species are kept as well. The importation of snakes from outside of Australia requires so many permits that it is almost impossible to do as well as being very expensive. The Australian Government is committed to protecting and conserving Australian native wildlife by regulating international trade. This helps to protect targeted species against overexploitation, and Australian ecosystems against the introduction of invasive species. The Australian Government supports the

105

efforts of other nations to protect their wildlife, by implementing the Convention on International Trade in Endangered Species of Wild Fauna and Flora. It is said that it easier to adopt a child from another country and bring that child into Australia than it is to bring in a snake.

Snakes on the property are mainly housed in wooden cages or plastic tubs. These enclosures are designed so that they have both hot and cold areas so that the snake can seek out whichever it desires. The temperature from one end of the enclosure to the other can vary from 20 C to 35 C.

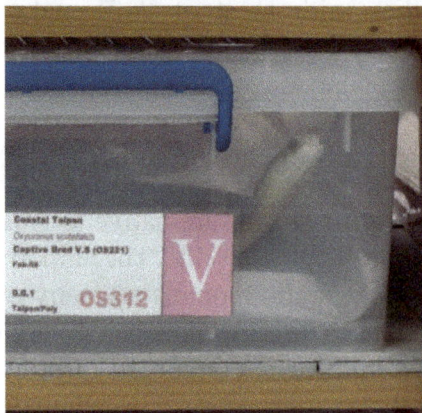

Various enclosures for the breeding of snakes and a Taipan in tub, awaiting milking.

Young snakes coming out of the incubator will go straight into their own tub but will go anything up to 14 days before they require feeding. Even with a snake only a few centimetres long care must be taken and smaller utensils are used when handling them.

A small percentage of the snakes on the property are house in well-designed outdoor pens. These enclosures also have areas where the snakes can either lie and bask in the sun or seek the cooler areas underground.

The greater majority of snake species lay eggs from which their young hatch. Depending on the species the offspring at a hatching can vary between 3 and 25. The eggs are collected from the breeding pens and placed in an incubator. The breeding season on the farm coincides with the breeding season of snakes in the wild. The temperature of incubator is kept at around 30 C with the humidity being kept well raised. After around 60 days in the incubator the eggs are ready to hatch. The period of time in the incubator can vary according to the species of snake being hatched. Most young snakes come equipped with an egg tooth on the top of their head and they utilize this to break through the shell.

Young snakes just beginning leave the egg.

A smaller percentage of snakes produce live young. The recorded largest hatching of live young is 98.

At Venom Supplies they only breed what is needed and they have no formal breeding programme. Juvenile snakes are much harder to handle than their adult counterparts and their bite can be just as lethal. Juvenile snakes usually feed on tadpoles and frogs whereas in captivity they are fed a foreign diet.

A captive bred snake usually has a longer life span than one in the wild with ages often exceeding 15 years. One of their snakes in an outdoor enclosure has an estimated age of 35 years.

With all these snakes comes the inherent problem of having to feed them. A snake diet consists of rodents and Venom Supplies raises all of its own food. In a specialized breeding shed they have 1000 breeding rats and mice from which they source all of their food. No new blood lines have been introduced into their rodent breeders since 2005, thus eliminating the possibility of disease. The rodents always have a supply of drinking water and a special high protein food mix available to them to assist in their growth rate.

Rodent breeding pens.

No live rodents are fed to the snakes with the rodents either having their necks broken or in the case of the smaller ones being euthanized with gas. The average size of a rodent litter is around 12 with litters being able to be produced every 21-30 days.

The size of the meal to be fed depends on the size of the snake receiving it. There are only about 12 snakes on the property that can digest a fully grown rat. It is a long held belief that the venom of a snake once injected into its prey, kills the prey and then breaks down the tissue of the prey so that it is almost digesting it from the inside out. Whereas a human or other animals have teeth to grind down their food a snake does not and so must rely upon other measures to assist with the food digestion. This theory has never been proven.

In Australia the only non venemous snakes are the python family but elsewhere throughout the world the proportion of non venemous snakes is quite large.

We come back now to the main purpose of Venom Supplies. The extraction of venom from the snakes either for research or the production of snake bite anti venom.

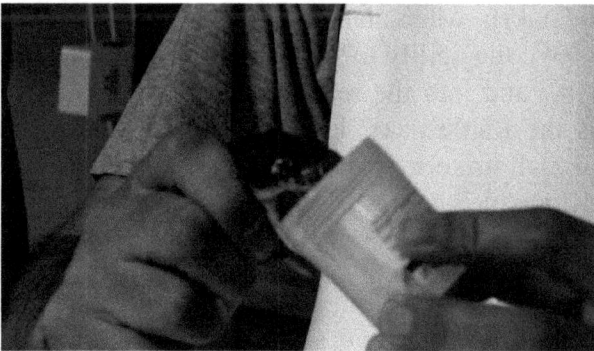

A snake in the process of being milked for its venom.

The venom is extracted from the snake by holding the snake just behind the head and forcing it to bite down on a thin membrane stretched over the top of a plastic container. As soon as the snake bites through the membrane its venom will flow from the fangs into the cup. Depending on the snake this venom can be very milky or almost like water. An average milking might bring around 2 milligrams of venom. The venom is then snap frozen with dry ice and can be kept in this state for up to 10 years.

While extracting venom from a snake can be done quite successfully by one person, two   persons are utilised on this farm. A pair of goggles and a thick rubber apron is all the protection that is used. Once a worker dons a pair of protective gloves they lose all feel for the snake. Gloves also impede the dexterity needed when handling the snake. As a snake is being milked its glands are   gently massaged by the fingers to increase the venom yield and gloves would impede this process. The element of danger in not wearing protective gloves tends to sharpen the focus on the task at hand and does not allow for complacency. The apron has become a must use item when milking snakes because of an accident where one of the snakes got free and managed to bite the handler on his stomach. It is also a great hygiene barrier. Extra care must be taken when handling the Viper species as these snakes have the ability to punch their fangs through the back of the jaw and into the restraining   finger. Other snakes, such as the Rattlesnake, have the ability to erect the fangs forward and strike in a head butt fashion. All Vipers have this ability which comes from the attribute of having 'hinged fangs'.

With the danger of working with these creatures every day there have only been two snake bites in the past 12 years. Following the correct procedures all of the time accounts for this low number.

Most of the venom extracted goes to research laboratories but some goes to a veterinary anti venom producer. bioCSL. They in turn inject the venom into animals. The standard bred horse (ex trotters) is the favoured animal in Australia while in the United States the sheep is the preferred animal). Horses are utilised for around 10 years and are then retired. They are exceptionally well looked after as they are the key to anti venom manufacture.

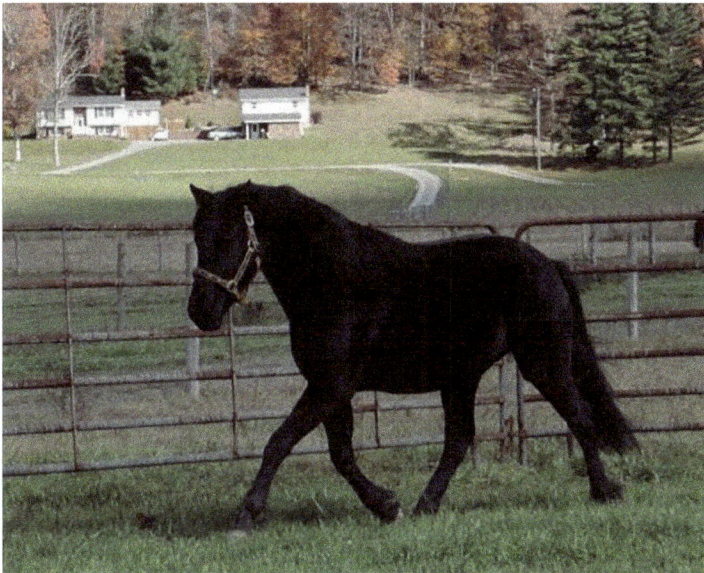

Horses are pastured in country Victoria and Queensland.

After quarantine, horses take around 9 months of sensitisation to venoms to become ready for the anti-venom programme. Sensitisation involves starting by introducing horses to small quantities of venoms, and the dose gradually increases as the horse immune system develops memory to the venoms.

The venoms are delivered in doses that include an adjuvant which binds the venom so the venom is released in the animal over an extended period of time. This ensures that the animals is not exposed to a large amount of venom all at once, and gives the immune system a better chance to develop antibodies to the venom.

It is the antibodies that are the active ingredient of anti-venom. When given to a patient, antibodies bind and effectively neutralise the venom- stop it from doing what it was going to do- like disrupt the nervous system, blood, or muscles for example. Anti-venom can't fix what the venom has already done though, so early treatment is imperative.

Once sensitised, horses can be dosed and bled on a seven week cycle, with Christmas off.

The horses are bled for the plasma component of their blood, in a manner similar to giving blood. The horse's blood is centrifuged or filtered, and the blood cells returned to the horse, with replacement fluid, while the antibody rich plasma component of the blood is collected.

Up to 15 litres of plasma can be collected from a horse in one bleed.

It takes at least 200 litres of plasma to start a batch of anti-venom production from horse plasma.

This plasma is the starting material for a fractionation process that isolates the antibodies from other blood proteins, and concentrates and purifies the antibodies to make anti venom.

Ant- venoms have a 3 year shelf life, after which they become less potent than the label claim of anti-venom units and therefore less effective. The anti-venom units in a vial of anti-venom was determined from the 'average' venom delivered from a bite of that particular species when the anti-venom was first developed.

The goal is to have any required anti venom available wherever in Australia it is likely to be needed.

This means that some anti-venom may expire prior to use if there are no envenomations requiring treatment in an area.

Hospitals and other medical facilities stock anti venoms required in their area.

Ant ivenoms can only be administered in a medical setting, as they are generally administered intravenously, and as they comprise animal proteins foreign to the human body, a chance for an allergic reaction exists.

Red back spiders are another sideline of Venom Supplies. They pay members of the public $1.00 per spider that they bring in. Some astute members of the community arrive with up to 200 red backs at a time and it can be quite a good little sideline for them. Red backs can be found almost anywhere in Australia. Because of the size of the spiders they are euthanized and the venom gland dissected out.

RED BACK SPIDER

The venom is extracted from the gland and then sold on to the anti-venom producer to be used as red back spider anti venom.

One other type of venom available from Venom Supplies is bee venom however all of their bee venom is sourced from a supplier in Romania with none available in Australia.

Anti-venom is a very expensive product to produce and does not have a very long expiry date. It is not a widely used product and most of what is produced is only replacing the out of date stock.

HAVE YOU EVER WONDERED?

WHAT THE GOVERNOR'S BUTLER'S DUTIES ARE WHEN HE REPORTS FOR WORK?

I visited the Vice Regal property in South Australia known as Government House, where I spoke at length with the Governor's personal butler, Troy Mason. South Australia's Government House is the oldest Government House in Australia and the second oldest continuously occupied home in Adelaide. It is set in grounds of 5.6 hectares of immaculately kept lawns, trees and perennial shrubs.

Although these grounds are virtually at the centre of a modern city it is not unusual to sight foxes running about within its confines. Giant pelicans have been observed to visit the water features scattered about the grounds and before the advent of modern security measures it was not unusual to sometimes find a city reveller sleeping it off under one of the large trees as the day staff arrived for work.

In an establishment such as this there are, what are termed, "back of house staff". The Butler and the staff surrounding him find themselves in this category. Some private households do have butlers and this is known as a "cool thing" by people who live in those circumstances. Being the Butler in a

Vice Regal establishment is the pinnacle for an aspiring butler. Quite a few homes in the USA have butlers but here they are often referred to as House Managers. Some up market hotels will offer a Butler to their well-heeled clients as an in-house service.

The duties of the Butler are wide and varied. It can begin with early morning starts depending on the movements for the day of the Governor and end in the early hours of the morning. Usually a start time of around 7 am is the norm when the Butler will touch base with the staff that may have been already working for a couple of hours and familiarize himself with what is happening during the day. Having control over the footmen and the kitchen staff includes such things as taking part in their employment interviews and continues through their training regime. His duties may involve seeing to the Governor's dry cleaning to routine maintenance of the huge crystal chandeliers or greeting a delivery person at the rear door.

Most butlers commence their careers as footmen and are often referred to as stewards. They have a very hands on roll, being in close daily contact with the Governor and his wife in a hospitality type position. Traditionally the footman will be the one who greets the Governor at the door when he returns from a function. As time goes by some of the more modern Governors have taken it upon themselves to let themselves in by the rear door.

When there is either Royalty or VIP guests staying at the house then the front door will always be manned by the footman when arrivals are expected.

The role of the butler, for centuries, has been that of the chief steward of a household, the   attendant entrusted with the care and serving of wine and other bottled beverages which in ancient times might have represented a considerable portion of the household's assets. A butler in a private household is often referred to as the House Manager, especially in the United States. In these   private roles the Butler will often travel with the family to their holiday destinations and overseas business trips.

The real-life modern butler attempts to be discreet and unobtrusive, friendly but not familiar, keenly anticipative of the needs of his or her employer, and graceful and precise in execution of duty. Butlers are the guardians of their employer's privacy and confidentiality. What happens in the privacy of their home stays within the confines of the home. One notable exception to this rule has been Paul Burrell who told all about his working relationship as the butler to Princess Dianna and went on to write books on the subject. It is the surest way of never again working in the industry.

With a residence the size of a Government House the services of many trades' people are   often required and it is the duty of the Butler to organize these tradesmen. He will build a rapport with them so that when work is required they will readily attend. The Butler also liaises with any company representatives that may have arranged to call on government House. The wine cellar at Government House is completely stocked with South Australian wines and it is the Butler's job to keep this fully stocked.

Even though a particular day may be quiet there is always the forward planning or the next large function that will not be very far away. There is the liaising with the Governor's private secretary as to when a function is coming up, how many guests are expected, which dining room will be utilized and how many staff will be required for it. Government House maintains a list of part time and casual employees that can be called on to work at these events and the Butler has to find out who will be available and roster available staff as required. It is not just a matter of ringing the employment agency and asking for some casual staff. All of these must be adequately trained to work at such an event and as such many will have come through various hospitality schools where training will have been provided. It could be very embarrassing for both the Governor and the State if untrained staff were employed. South Australia has the only Government accredited butler training school in the world. Students are trained in household management, financial, household, organizing contract workers and event organization. Butlers are required to be perfectionists and have a passion for service.

In a Vice Regal household the Butler will refer to the Governor as Your Excellency, usually first thing in the morning and when other people are around. Dropping back to call him Sir is usually when he is alone with the Governor and this is quite acceptable. Even though they will develop a close working relationship protocol must always be observed.

With the advent of some modern Governors coming from civilian ranks they are coming into a job for which they have had no formal training. They will rely upon a close working relationship with the Butler to ease them into their new role. Depending on the circumstances sometimes there is less than a week changeover time   between Governors and this can place a strain on the incoming Governor as well as the household staff. Getting used to changes within the household that a new   Governor might bring can be too much at times for the staff and they will leave to seek employment elsewhere.

It is good to note that at the South Australian Government House the chauffeur, cook and butler have been there from 21 to 35 years. During this time they have seen many Governors come and go but still they remain. This says a lot about the working environment of an establishment such as this.

One interesting thing of note was that back in 1862 a Police Inspector was shot dead inside Government House. The Governor of the day was holding an auction to sell off some of his furniture before travelling back to England and there was a large crowd present. A former police officer gained entry to the grounds as he was well known to the police on duty at the gate. When the chance arose he took a pistol that he had concealed on his body and shot the police inspector in the head, killing him instantly. It appears that he had a long standing grievance with the inspector. The shooter was found guilty and later hanged at the Adelaide Gaol.

Even to this day, when something strange happens within the house, the staffs blame it on the ghost of the dead inspector.

Butlers are coming back in vogue and Troy thinks that they are becoming more popular than ever before. A good butler in Australia can earn between sixty to one hundred thousand dollars with figures over two hundred thousand being touted in some overseas establishments.

There have been many humouress things that have happened over the years but because of the nature of the establishment and without mentioning certain names it would be unfair to go into them.

One, unconfirmed report, is that a member of the British Royal family, while staying at the house found himself wandering the corridors, late at night and stumbling across some of the staff playing poker. It will not be confirmed or denied that he still had the shirt on his back when he later returned to his room. (It is a well-known fact that members of the Royal Family are not in the habit of carrying money in their pockets)

HAVE YOU EVER WONDERED?

HOW AND WHY A FAMILY'S LIFE MIGHT CHANGE WHEN THEY UNDERTAKE A SEA CHANGE.

A Sea Change is when people move from the city to start a new life, generally in a coastal town or sometimes even in some secluded location right next to the ocean.

Where would you rather live and bring up a family.

A Sea Change is not to be mistaken for a Tree Change where people move from the city into the hills or the country further afield. They may find themselves in a small country town or on acreage, well away from the nearest neighbours.

Depending on the individual, isolation can be as hard to bear as a busy city location.

A national task force has been looking at this phenomena and they have projected that up to a million people could be making this change in the next 15 years in Australia alone. The main cause attributed to this is the demands of city life and the stress that it can cause.

The change can be a smooth transition from one life to another, but on the other hand it came become an absolute nightmare.

An unhappy Sea Change can leave a family feeling lonely and isolated, cut off from their family and friends. Anyone contemplating such a change in their lifestyle should really do their research as to just what they are looking for and whether the change will justify the   sacrifices they make.

To see the effects of a family making a dramatic sea change we chose Allison and Glen Newton from Merimbula, a small town near the east coast of Australia between Sydney and Melbourne. They made the dramatic change in their lives when they moved with their three children from a populated area to the town of Karumba on the coast of the Gulf of Carpentaria in 2001. Karumba is a small town with a population of around 518 compared to Merimbula's of almost 9000.   It is situated over 2000 kilometres from the Queensland capital of Brisbane and over 70 kilometres from its nearest town of Normanton, itself a relatively small town.

Their first glimpse of this town was when they visited for a short time while on a holiday around Australia. They called in and stayed at the caravan park in the town for a short time and fell in love with the town. After the return to their home, thoughts of Karumba were still in their minds. They decided to travel back up there and complete the final two terms of the school year.

The Newtons arrived and settled into the caravan park for a month. While there they again stayed at the caravan park and did some work there.

This time gave them an insight into the lifestyle of the people of the town and the schooling available for their three children. They also came across a business that was for sale. Ferryman Cruises catered for the tourist population that visits the town during Australia's winter months when temperatures in the southern states can be quite miserable. The business operated fishing charters and crocodile and bird spotting cruises into the gulf and close by rivers. With an abundance of salt water crocodiles in the area and many bird species that are difficult to find anywhere else the Newtons realized that this was going to be too good to pass up.

With their minds made up they made their way back towards home thinking only of the opportunity that lay before them.

Glen had been a mechanic at Merimbula and had suffered an injury that was preventing him going back to his trade. He had a liking for fishing and so set about obtaining the necessary licences that would permit him to operate the business back in Karumba. Once this was done they rented out their home and set about changing their life.

When they arrived back in Karumba they took over Ferryman Cruises and its one boat. Glen obtained his skipper's certificate and Allison obtained hers later.

The boat they now owned was licensed to carry fifty passengers and they set about building up their business by purchasing another boat. This enabled them to run the ever popular sunset cruises out into the gulf and also the croc spotting and bird watching tours.

Soon a third boat was purchased that enabled them to diversify the business into fishing charters.

As with all small businesses it was not always smooth sailing but with perseverance the business has flourished. Both Glen and Allison are very hands on when it comes to the business and their diversifications cater for the great many tourists who visit the region each year. They have grown the business to such a degree that now bookings are almost always needed.

The change they had made to their lives was never about money but gaining a better lifestyle for their family. The children, one of whom had a learning disability, flourished in their new, much smaller school. The only disadvantage came when the children reached secondary school level and they had to board away from Karumba and attend school at Charters Towers. This however did not curb the children's learning ability and they continued to flourish.

It was not a hard decision to make the move and looking back now, 12 years later, there are absolutely no regrets. The children have become less obsessed with themselves and less selfish, developing more respect for other people around them and the community. There is much more freedom for the children and they have learnt to laugh and have fun. The pressure of living close to big cities was no longer with them.

As the children grew older they have taken a greater interest in the business and often help out on the various cruises with their parents. The eldest child has now graduated from university and the second one is about to commence. Their youngest now has a mathematics scholarship at his high school. Whether the children's success would have happened if they had not made the change is open for conjecture but the Newton's believe that it has greatly improved the way the children live their lives.

The Newtons and Ferryman Cruises are a great example of how a Sea Change can alter a family's perspective of life. They did not rush their decision to make the change but once the idea was formed there was no looking back.

For every family, such as the Newtons who make a success of their change there are many who fail and are miserable. Research appears to be the key to making such a change and being prepared to fit in with a new community.

Being able to make the move and not have to worry about employment in your new surroundings will make the transition much easier. Making a sea change is not an easy thing to do and the less worry you have upon arriving will help greatly. Proper research will pay off in the long run even though at the time it might seem tedious. Having all family members happy with the change is an important feature of a successful change.

A successful sea change will make one's life much better as long as it is done for the right reasons. Leaving the hustle and bustle of big city living behind and settling into a small country community can alleviate all the stress in one's life.

HAVE YOU EVER WONDERED?

HOW AND WHY AN AUTOPSY IS PERFORMED?

Have you ever wondered what takes place behind the scenes in the Forensic Science building when an autopsy has to be performed on a body?

First we must find out why and when an autopsy is performed as most people when they die are not subject to this.

A post mortem is carried out at the direction of the Coroner and is usually required to ascertain the precise cause of death of the person. Where a person's treating doctor supplies a Death Certificate the post mortem in not usually required.

A post mortem will be carried out as soon as practicable so that the deceased person's body can be released to relatives for burial.

A major benefit of a post mortem is that it will provide detailed information about the person's previous medical condition prior to death and will give an understanding of the various factors that may have contributed to the death. This information can be very important to family members trying to come to terms with the death.

Now, what is an autopsy?

The study of an autopsy begins with two basic assumptions.

1. The life of the individual is of the highest value; and
2. The deceased person is to be treated with reverence.

An autopsy, often referred to as a post mortem examination, is a medical procedure that consists of a thorough examination of a corpse to determine the cause and manner of death and to evaluate any disease or injury that may be present. An autopsy is carried out by a specialized medical practitioner called a pathologist.

Autopsies are either performed for legal or medical reasons. A forensic autopsy is performed when the cause of death may be a criminal mater, while a clinical or academic autopsy is performed to find the medical cause of death where that cause is either unknown or uncertain. In simple terms, "Why did life pass from this body?" It is an evaluation of an individual's death and the circumstances surrounding it.

An autopsy is carried not to benefit the deceased but to benefit the living.

The essence of an autopsy is working backwards from the one known factor; a death has occurred.

Autopsies can be split into two categories. Sometimes an external examination can be sufficient and on other   occasions the body needs to be dissected and the internal organs examined. Once the internal autopsy is complete the body is reconstituted by sewing it back together.

The Egyptians were one of the first civilizations to practice the removal of internal organs of humans while Giovanni Morgagni; (1682-1771) is celebrated as the father of modern anatomical pathology.

How is it carried out?

A body usually arrives at the examining office in a body bag or evidence sheet. These items are only used once to prevent contamination.

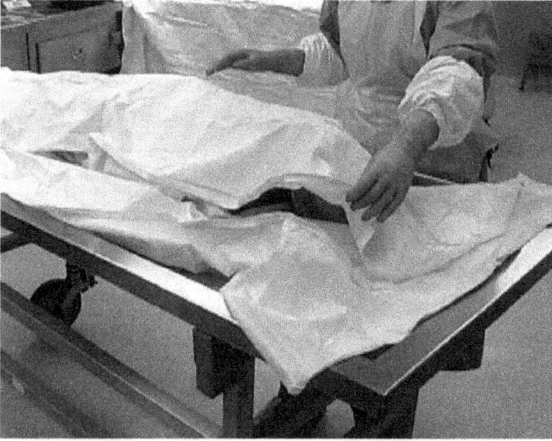

The body is removed from the body bag.

Before the body bag is opened everyone present should be suited up for protection from airborne pathogens. The body would have been suitably tagged at the scene and these tags should be identified so that there can be no case of mistaken identity.

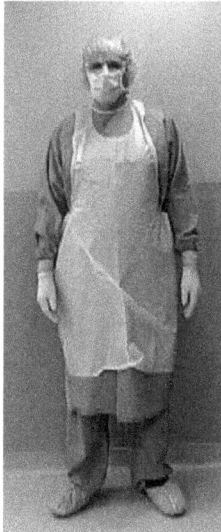

Proper protection of the pathologist and all assistants is essential.

At many institutions the person designated for the handling, cleaning and moving of the body is called an   Anatomical Pathology Technologist although this can vary between   institutions.   This person will also assist the pathologist with the disembowelling of the deceased and body reconstruction afterwards. When the body is first received it will be photographed. The examiner will then note the clothing and   position on the body before they are removed. Next, any evidence such as residues, flakes of paint or other material is collected from the outer body. Some evidence may not be visible to the naked eye and an ultra violet light may be used to find these. Samples of hair, nails and the like are then taken and the body may be x-rayed. Once this is all done the body will be removed from the bag and undressed. Any surface wounds will be examined at this stage. The external examination of a deceased is a focused head to toe examination of the body from the hair on the top of the head to the toe nails. As much time can be spent on the external as the internal examination. Most pathologists use a systematic examination process of the deceased so as to not overlook any area of the body.

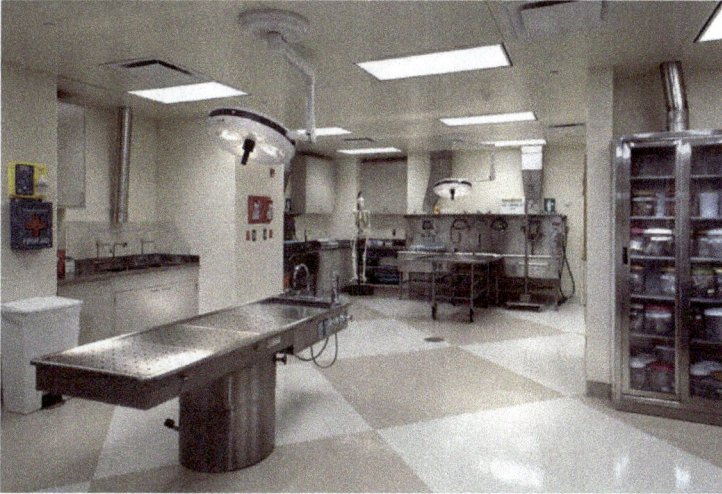

A MODERN AUTOPSY ROOM

The body is now ready for cleaning, weighing and measured for an internal exam.

A hand held voice recorder or examination sheet are then utilized for recording the ethnicity, sex, age, hair colour and length, eye colour and other distinguishing features such as birth marks, scars or moles etc.

A body block, (plastic or rubber brick) is then placed under the back causing the arms and neck to fall backwards while pushing the chest upward making it easier to cut open.

A person's skin is technically an organ. It is the organ that is most carefully assessed during the external examination. The skin acts as an outward sentinel for deep injuries or diseases within the body.

The body is now ready for the internal examination to begin.

There are three different types of approaches available.

Sometimes a large and deep Y shaped incision is made commencing at the tips of each shoulder and running down the front of the chest to meet at the lower point of the breast bone.

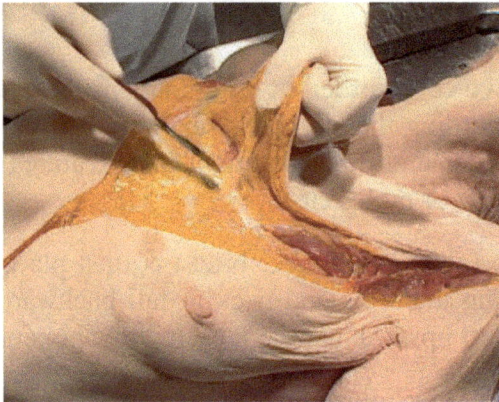

Another method is to make a T shaped incision from the tips of both shoulders and horizontally across the body in the region of the collar bone and meeting at the middle of the breast bone.

The last method is to make a single cut from the middle of the neck (in the region of the Adam's apple on a male body).

In all three of the above methods the cut is then extended down to the pubic bone missing the belly button to the left or right side.

There is little or no bleeding at this point as the only blood pressure is that caused by gravity. In the case of drowning however, bleeding can be quite profuse.

An electric bone saw is now used to cut open the chest cavity. This will cause quite a bit of dust residue and shears or a scalpel blade may be used as an alternative. The said tool is then used to cut through the ribs on the lateral side of the chest cavity to allow to sternum and attached ribs to be lifted out as one. This is done to allow the heart and lungs to be examined without fear of damaging them. A scalpel is then used to cut away any remaining flesh that is still attached to the chest late. The lungs and heart are now fully exposed. At the completion of the autopsy the breast plate will be replaced.

The organs are then removed in one of two ways. They are either removed as one large mass or divided into groups of organs. There is no right or wrong way to do this. The aim is to perform a complete autopsy and to provide a detailed description of that autopsy.

We will deal with one of these methods.

First the pericardial sac is opened to view the heart. Blood for analysis may be removed from the inferior vena cava or the pulmonary veins. Before the heart is removed the pulmonary artery is opened in order to search for any blood clots.

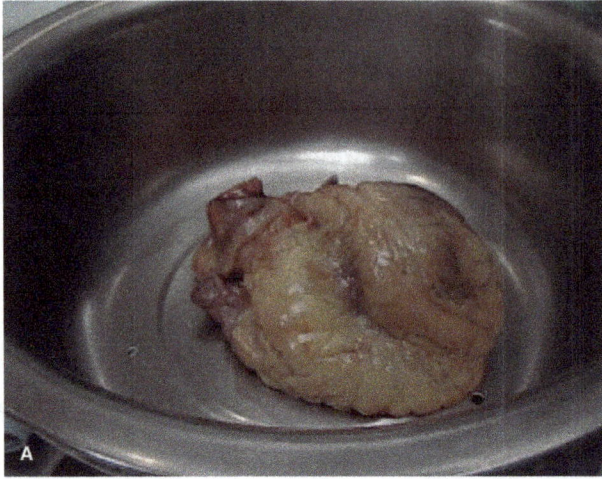

The heart, like all organs, is weighed. Increased weight of the heart can indicate hypertensive heart disease or numerous other conditions such a cardiomyopathy. The heart is a specialized muscle that increases in weight the more work it is required to do. High blood pressure can increase the size of the heart because of the extra work load.

The heart is then removed by cutting the inferior vena cava, the pulmonary veins, the aorta and pulmonary artery and the superior vena cava. This method will leave the aortic arch intact and this makes things easier for the embalmer. The left lung is now easily accessible and can be removed by cutting the bronchus artery and vein at the point that they enter the lung cavity. The right lung can now be readily removed in the same way. The abdominal organs can be removed, one by one after first examining their relationships and vessels.

The various organs are then examined, weighed and slices of tissue samples are taken. Every major blood vessel is cut open and inspected at this stage.

The stomach and intestinal contents are now examined and weighed. This can assist in finding the cause and time of death due to the natural passage of food through the bowel during digestion.

The body block that was earlier used to elevate the body is now used to elevate the head. To examine the brain an incision is made from behind one ear, over the crown of the head, to a point behind the other ear. The scalp is then pulled away from the skull in two directions. The front section is pulled down over the face while the rear section is pulled down over the back of the neck. The skull is now cut in a circle with an electric saw allowing the cap to be lifted of exposing the brain. After the brain is examined in its cavity the connections to the spinal cord and cranial nerves are severed allowing the brain to be lifted out for closer examination. If the brain needs to be preserved prior to examination it is placed in a large container of formalin. As well as preserving the brain this also makes it firmer allowing easier handling without corrupting the tissue.

With the autopsy complete it is now time to reconstitute the body in preparation for viewing by relatives and the burial. At this stage we have in front of us an open and empty chest cavity, an open skull with the scalp flaps pulled over the face and back of the neck.

In most cases the body cavity is lined with cotton wool or some other appropriate material and the organs are placed in a plastic bag and returned to the body cavity. It was once a common practice for items such as the brain to be placed in the chest cavity and the skull cavity filled with crumpled newspaper to fill the void. This practice is not often carried out these days. The chest plate is then replaced and the chest flaps are closed and sewn into position. The skull cap is then replaced and the scalp stitched into place. The body may then be wrapped in a shroud and it is common for relatives not to be able to tell the procedure has been done at a viewing.

HAVE YOU EVER WONDERED?

HOW A CRAYFISH MAKES IT FROM THE OCEAN FLOOR TO A DINNER PLATE HALF WAY ACROSS THE WORLD?

Life begins for these small creatures in an egg sac under their mother's body. After a period of days in this position a baby crayfish is born. We are going to tell the story of the young crayfish from his early beginnings to his demise in one of the restaurants of the world.

After dropping to the seabed along with many of his siblings, he finds that he is not alone. From this point on it was a matter of survival. There are many predators in the ocean that would like to end the young crayfish's life. The worst of these is the octopus and he needs to steer well clear of these. The lucky ones, find a safe place to hide, and managed to avoid their enemies until finally they grow into a good size crayfish.

The next chapter in this story is when the young Cray finds himself trapped in a steel Cray pot that has been dropped to the ocean floor by a crayfish boat. The pot would have contained a fish head or some other form of meaty bait to entice the cays inside.

A Cray boat averages about 16 metres in length and can be worth approximately $600,000. They can be licensed to work with around the average of 90 pots and at a cost of $55,000 a pot, is a considerable investment. With its skipper and crew member, it had been out for almost 9 hours and had taken 85 pots from the water, retrieved what cays might be inside them, re baited each pot and returned it to the ocean floor for the following days catch. The position of each pot is marked with a marker buoy and noted on the boat's GPS system. The day's journey had used almost 500 litres of fuel and even with a government rebate; this was a costly day's work.

The Cray boat continued its days work before heading back into port with many kilograms of live cays in its tank. Before reaching port, all of the cays have been placed in smaller plastic tubs for easy transportation.

The boat's skipper uses his mobile phone to communicate with some of the crayfish buyers who would be waiting at the wharf to purchase his days catch. Some boat skippers would sell on a rotation basis to the buyers knowing that most prices offered would be about the same and that this way would keep all of the buyers onside. However, this skipper wanted the best price he could get for his catch and after four phone calls decided to sell his catch at a price of $68.00 a kilo.

As the boat stopped the plastic tubs holding the cays are lifted out of the boat and loaded onto a small trolley. After a brief ride on the trolley, the tubs are lifted onto an electronic weighing machine and then loaded into the back of a buyer's refrigerated van alongside other tubs of crayfish that have been purchased from other fishing boats.

The buyer then hands the boat skipper a note outlining the number of kilograms of his catch. When all of the boats have returned and knowing that he would not be making any other purchases, the buyer would commence the long trip to the fish factory.

Arriving at the fish factory the buyer unloaded his catch onto a conveyor belt and the tubs are wheeled inside. Here workers lifted the Crayfish from the tubs and sort them by size into steel cages in large vats of clear seawater.

Crays after being sorted and waiting to be packed.

The seawater is trucked into the fish factory daily to maintain a good quality. The recent   arrivals at the   factory are sorted according to their size and placed in one of several large salt water vats that are gradually chilled to varying temperatures and a sedative added. As the crayfish venture further along the production line the water becomes colder until it reaches about 6 C. By this time the combination of the sedative and the water temperature has slowed the crayfish's metabolism so that they are easier to handle and will travel better.

CRAYS WAITING TO BE PACKED

The workers in the factory commence to take the crayfish out of the cages and pack them into foam boxes   according to their size. For the smaller 600-gram crayfish they are packed, 36 to a box, along with wood   shavings and an ice pack before the lid is securely taped into position for transportation.

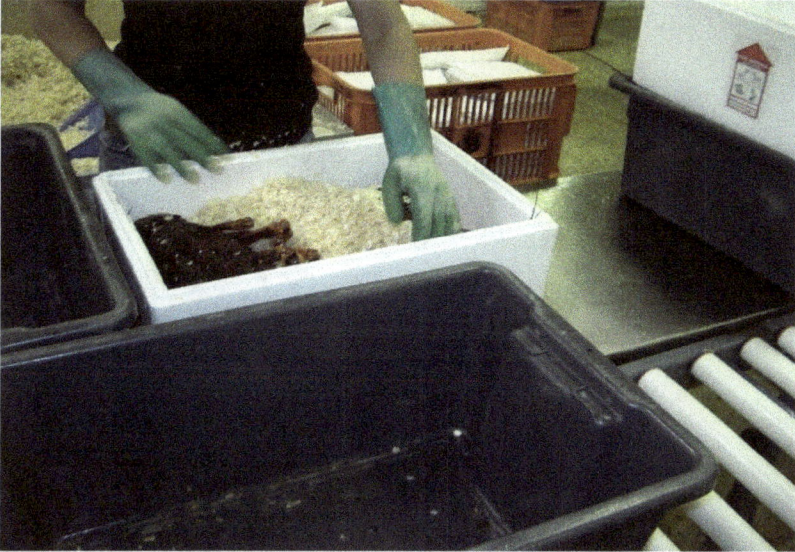

CRAYS BEING PACKED READY FOR TRANSPORTA-
TION

This nights packing were all headed to China. As the size of
the Cray increases so there are less to a box. The sealed boxes
are then loaded into the rear of another van for the trip to the
international airport. Here they will be loaded onto a freighter
for their long trip to China where the majority of crayfish are
sent.

The cost of freighting Crayfish to China is about $7.00 a kil-
ogram and so from the amount of $68.00 the buyer paid to
the boat skipper the end cost is beginning to rise dramatically
considering the journey that has been undertaken from the
ocean floor only three days previously.

Upon reaching China, the crayfish are starting to arouse from
their long sleep and they find themselves at a fish market
where there is a lot of noise and yelling. As the crayfish are
on sold to their final purchasers, they will find themselves
being taken on another van ride to a back alley behind a res-

taurant. Here they will be unloaded and taken inside to be placed into large glass tanks where other crayfish are moving about. The crayfish by this time has recovered from the previously administered sedative and would be gazing out into the restaurant onto the dining area. At this point of time, patrons at the restaurant would be choosing the crayfish they desired. The waiter would lift the crayfish out of the tank and carry him to the rear kitchen.

Sadly, the crayfish's journey has ended.

A strange twist comes at the end of the crayfish's life when he comes back out into the restaurant on a large dinner plate alongside his old enemy the octopus.

HAVE YOU EVER WONDERED?

WHAT THE DAY MIGHT BRING FOR A ZOO KEEP-ER?

We must first acknowledge what motivates someone to become a zookeeper. They are a person who has a   passion for animals and who usually has some qualification in animal husbandry, experience with animals though a sanctuary or wildlife park or with a varying array of domestic or farm animals. Currently various courses are conducted in zoology, animal husbandry or in vet nursing that are becoming a prerequisite for a life as a zookeeper. Zookeeper positions are very much sought after and breaking into this field can be quite hard.

A zookeeper is the number one person in the wheel of animal zoo husbandry. It is not the zoo director, zoo vet or the head keeper. They play an important part in the scheme of things but their job is directly influenced by the professionalism of the zoo keeper.

A zoo keeper works very hard every day caring for the   animals in their care. They help maintain animal health through proper nutrition and medication, train animals for behaviours that help staff asses their health, study animal behaviour, work to aid in the conservation of endangered species, educate the public about animals and much more.

What image the public form in their minds and the actual work of the zookeeper can be quite different.

Zoos are divided into various sections such as primates, carnivores, children's section etc. and zoo keepers are allotted to one of these sections. Zookeepers can move around between the sections but more often than not will remain with one group.

A zookeeper's day usually starts early when they check on the animals in their care. These animals have usually spent the night confined to their night quarters. Small portions of food are usually given out at this time to   enable the keeper to develop a rapport with the animals and be able to get close enough for a quick inspection for any possible injury or sickness.

 At some zoos the keepers will collect samples of urine and faeces from the animals as these are valuable tools for the scientists who collect data to determine hormone levels and detect any potential sickness or disease early.

Then the not so glamorous task of cleaning out the display areas, from which the public can view the animals, is carried out. This can involve removing the animal droppings and any old food that may be left from the previous day. A good sweep, rake or hose down will usually complete this task.

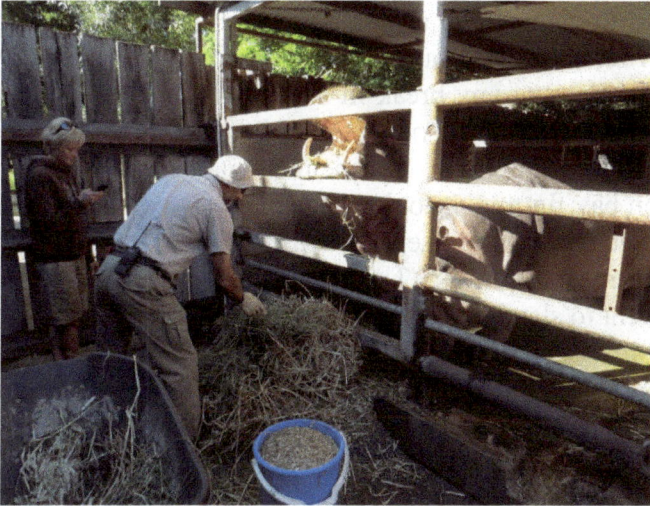

In some circumstances, such as the giraffes, where their food is hung high in the air to try and emulate their natural feeding habits this will be done before the animals are let out.

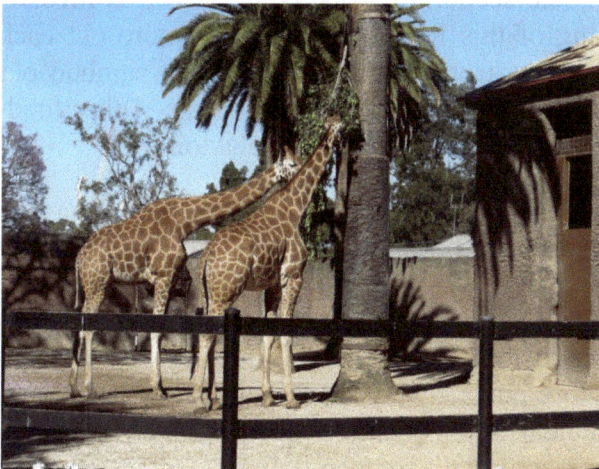

This is also done in areas where once the animals are out on display it would not be safe for the keepers to enter the enclosure to take in food. A visual check of perimeter fencing including electric fences in case something has happened during the night is always carried out. It does not take much for a branch to come down across a moat or fall onto an electric fence wire, shorting it out. Animals are very clever and will take advantage of any break in security for a chance at their freedom. One instance of this is when a Siamese monkey managed to jump from its enclosure and climb a nearby Moreton bay fig tree. It took 5 keepers, an extension ladder, and a net and tranquiliser darts from the vet along with 2 hours to recapture him. The tranquiliser darts did their job but it went to sleep at the top of the tree.

The keepers then have the task of cleaning out the night quarters where the animals have been confined for up to 14 hours. As you can imagine this could be a very messy situation and has to be done daily. These are tasks done out of the public eye in the back rooms and tunnels behind the display areas.

Zoos have to search everywhere for the varying food requirements of their exhibits and even have started small farms and allotments at which to grow the necessary items. A complete section of workers at the zoo is involved in the gathering of this food. Some will venture out each day to gather leaves from particular trees or to bamboo plantations specifically planted for the zoo's needs. Other food such as the meat is trucked in daily from abattoirs

Many of the animals at a zoo have special dietary needs and the keeper must be abreast of what they need and administer the specified doses of medication along with the meals. A zoo keeper acts as a vet nurse and at times is required to administer treatment via syringe. This is where their constant daily close contact with the animal can assist. Even a carnivore such as a lion or tiger will rub its side up against a cage while reacting with somebody that it knows and trusts making a quick jab with a syringe a better proposition that the animal being darted with a blowgun.

One of the foremost things on worth keeping's mind is the aspect of animal security. All cages and doors have to be locked at all times for the well-being of both the animals, keepers and the public. While all keepers have their own keys when they work around the cages of the carnivores, only one key can be used in a lock thus eliminating the possibility of a keeper going into a cage where the previous keeper may have just let an animal into.

An interesting story is told of the Siberian tiger that died in its enclosure. The keepers removed it and it was frozen for later research. A couple of the keepers arranged the animal so that it was facing towards the door of the freezer room. Not long after this the freezer door was opened by some zoo members attending a function only to come face to face with this huge Siberian tiger. The story goes that the members left the vicinity very quickly. There were later repercussions for the zoo keepers who carried out the prank.

Keepers usually work by themselves but sometimes another will help if they have finished early or for some specific task.

The close daily contact between animal and keeper can form a bond and some animals almost become like domestic pets in their attachment. This is a good reason why keepers will often stay in the one section for many years. The down side to this is that all animals have a lifespan that will almost certainly expire within the zoo confines. The keepers have to constantly deal with losing an animal or bird with which they have bonded. Birds seem to have the longest longevity of life and are one of the few that will outstay the keepers. As can be imagined, many lives are lost to a zoo community during the period of a year but on the upside, quite a few new lives commence within the zoo perimeter. Breeding programmes are carried out in all zoos as this is the only way that many of the species will survive. Some species are on the verge of extinction in the wild, mainly through destruction of their habitat or poaching. Many species have been lost to us already and it is the job of zoos to try and combat this.

In the afternoon, a reverse procedure is instigated to ensure that the animals return to their night quarters and are safely locked away. Animals can be creatures of habit and get to know that food is in the night quarters for them and most are very happy to return there.

Once the animals are safely secured for the night, the keeper's day ends.

While it is a rewarding job being a zoo keeper it is not as glamorous as it might seem. Because animals have to be cared for every single day the keepers will work a seven day roster. This work is often outside in rain and heat and all sorts of other weather. It can be a very manual job with them having to carry heavy containers of food to the enclosures. It can also be a very dangerous job as most wild animals can bite, scratch, kick and spread disease.

Even animals as cuddly as the Panda are not treated without due respect as even they can inflict serious injury.

In spite of all of this you will find that the majority of zoo keepers really love their job and could not envisage working in any other environment. The majority of them have never wanted to do anything else.

HAVE YOU EVER WONDERED?

HOW A BODY IS CREMATED?

In most civilized countries, the cremation of a body is very strictly controlled by the authorities. Legislation is enacted to safeguard the family of the deceased, the funeral director, the crematorium and the rights of the deceased.

While some procedures may vary, we will cover the most common practice throughout the world.

After a person has died the family of that person deal with a funeral director. If the wish is for a cremation, the funeral director will apply for a Cremation Certificate, usually from an organisation as the Registrar of Births, Deaths and Marriages.

When approval is granted, a copy is usually faxed to the chosen crematorium. An official cremation can only be carried out in an approved crematorium and not on a bonfire at a beach.

The funeral director will liaise with the family and prepare the body for cremation. A cremation cannot be carried out if an immediate relative objects unless it is specified in the Last Will and Testament of the deceased.

The funeral director will utilise a coffin that is constructed out of wood or a derivative of wood. This coffin will be lined with an impervious layer to prevent the leakage of any bodily fluids. A nameplate will be attached to the outside of the coffin bearing the surname and a Christian name of the deceased and the coffin will then be sealed transport it to the place where the service will be held or to the crematorium, depending on the circumstances. Some families like to have a service somewhere other than where the cremation will take place and some crematoriums do not have facilities for a service to be held there.

When the coffin eventually arrives at the crematorium it must have in place the nameplate and be accompanied by the cremation permit and an identity sheet signed by somebody who knew the deceased. There must also be an instruction sheet from the person who requested the permit indicating what is to be done with the remains. The last piece of paperwork is from the funeral director stating that the contents of the coffin will not explode when subject to heat. Funeral directors must remove any items, such as pace makers from the body before sealing the coffin to prevent such explosions and therefore   possible damage to the cremator.

The crematorium upon receiving the body will generate two identification labels. One is attached to the coffin and the other remains on the trolley used to transport the coffin.

If the service is to be held in the crematorium, then when the body is lowered from sight at the end of the service it goes onto a trolley to be transported to the cremation area. It is often believed by those watching the coffin being lowered that it is going straight down into the cremator but this is not the case.

The recommended temperature at which a cremator operates is between 750 and 850 Celsius. The length of time taken for a body to be cremated is usually between 1.5 and 2 hours depending on the body size. A body with a lot of fat will burn faster than a lean muscular body. Emissions from the cremator are strictly controlled by the local authorities in regular air quality checks.

CREMATORS AT WORK

Some cremators are automatic in that the body will be inserted automatically and the burn time regulated according to size. The operator cans usually over ride this if the need arises. Modern cremators have the coffin going in one end and the remains leaving via the other but this can vary according to location.

Before the coffin is inserted into the cremator, all metal handles are removed. Most crematoriums will have an arrangement with a reputable scrap metal dealer who will collect the metal handles and sign a certificate. This certifies that they will be disposed of in a way that they cannot be recycled. Any plastic handles will remain on the coffin and will be destroyed by the heat.

At the end of the cremation, the ashes will come out into a meal hopper and take a further 1-2 hours to cool down. Once this is done any items such as joint replacements and coffin nails will be removed and disposed of to a scrap metal dealer to be dealt with as outlined above. There will be mainly ash and some bone fragments left and sometimes fragments of the coffin.

At this point, a granulator is used to reduce everything to a powder and then place the powder into an urn. Most remains weigh less than 4 kilograms.

A label is then attached to the bottom of the urn and a second identical label is inserted into the urn with the ashes before it is sealed. This is done so that the ashes can always be identified later if the need should ever arise.

The sealed urn is then ready for the family to collect or to be disposed of according to prior arrangements.

It is possible for a family of the deceased to observe the insertion of the coffin into the cremator from behind a glass window. This is mainly done because of religious beliefs.

Cremation is becoming more popular than burial with the gap between the two ever increasing. One of the reasons for this is the cost factor where cremation can be half the cost of a burial.

In countries, such as Japan, where the cremation rate is around 99%, the lack of ground space has a big bearing on the high percentage. Other countries, such as Greece, the cremation rate is very low with laws only being recently passed to allow cremation. Religious beliefs are the cause of this.

When you think that there are more people alive on the earth today than have ever died previously, this method of disposing of a body is going to become a necessity in the future.

The overriding fact is that there are not enough Crematoriums and that most of them are in capital cities. Persons dying in the country will continue to be buried until more crematoriums are built.

HAVE YOU EVER WONDERED?

What it takes to put a top rate sporting team on the field?

We chose two top sporting clubs from opposite sides of the globe to see what it takes, behind the scenes, to be able to field teams in their respective codes of sport.

Manchester City Football Club, from England, the reigning premier league champions for 2012 and the Adelaide Football Club from Australia, who have just finished third in the Australian Football League's 2012 season.

The first thing that you realise after going behind the scenes at these two great clubs is that only a small portion of the revenue that keeps them going comes from football. Sponsorship plays a big part in putting a team on the sporting arena. Both clubs have staff whose job it is to procure new sponsors and also see to the needs of the existing sponsors. Without sponsors, clubs such as these two would not be able to field a team each week. There are in the vicinity of thirty four individual sponsors on five separate levels of sponsorship that support the Adelaide Football Club throughout the year. Manchester City prefer to use the name "Partners" when they refer to their sponsors and there are fourteen of them with the largest being Etihad Airlines who have recently signed a deal rumoured to be worth around four hundred million dollars.

With Manchester City first formed in 1880 as the Ardwick Association Football Club by St Marks Church, only taking the current name in 1894 and the Adelaide Football Club being formed in 1990 you see there is a great divide in the history of the respective clubs.

Ownership of the two clubs differs in that Manchester City is owned by an individual person, Sheik Mansour Bin Zayed Al Nahan with a personal wealth of around seventeen billion dollars and a family wealth of about one trillion dollars. The Adelaide Football Club is owned by the South Australian National Football League which has a total equity of around eighty four million dollars. Quite a gap between the two clubs. Private ownership has been tried, unsuccessfully, on three occasions in Australia.

Manchester City has a staff of around 300 compared to the Adelaide Football Club with 80 full time staff. Both clubs come from cities that support two teams in their respective leagues. As such there is fierce across town rivalry between the supporters of the two clubs. Unfortunately the rivalry between Manchester City and Manchester United is so strong that the supporters have to be separated when the two teams play each other, or else the game would never get under way.

This is done by the allocation of seating in different sections of the ground for each team's supporters and a strong police and official presence, both inside and outside the ground.

While the rivalry between the Adelaide Football Club and its co city rivals, Port Adelaide is fierce it does not require the above measures to be taken to ensure the game goes on.

Manchester City draws its supporters from Manchester, a city of around 2.6 million people while the Adelaide Football Club takes its members from the 1.3 million people living in South Australia. Adelaide has forty five thousand members and Manchester has thirty six thousand season ticket holders. In 2011 Adelaide drew an average of just over thirty five thousand supporters to each game while Manchester regularly fills its forty seven thousand seat stadium for home matches.

AAMI Stadium, ADELAIDE

ETIHAD Stadium, MANCHESTER

The Adelaide Football Club operates within a thirty million dollar budget of which nine million dollars is paid to the forty five players within its playing group. Compare this to Manchester City where one of the players earns approximately thirteen million dollars and the lowest paid players on the team roster earn in excess of eight hundred thousand dollars. This team competes in a league where the average player payment is around eight and a half million dollars each year. If one was to attend a normal training session at any one of the clubs in the English First Division they would see players rolling up in Porsches and Ferraris. In 2012 only seven players, in the Australian Football League, of the total of six hundred and eighty four, earned in excess of one million dollars with the average for all listed players in the vicinity of two hundred and forty thousand dollars. This average is expected to top three hundred thousand dollars by 2016. Teams in the Australian Football League must fit the salaries of all their team members under a salary cap. The payment limit is set by the governing body each year and it is designed to help bridge the gap between the rich and not so rich clubs.

Without a salary cap the more affluent teams would be able to contract all of the better players available, leaving the less affluent clubs with only a lesser quality player for their team. Teams are required to spend at least 92% of their salary cap each year. Very heavy fines and sanctions are imposed on any teams breaching the conditions of the salary cap. By coupling this condition with the lower finishing teams from the previous year obtaining first choices of players in the new season's draft, it tends to level out the competition for the coming year.

If we go to the other side of the globe we find there is no maximum amount a player can earn with Manchester City budgeting around 500 million pound for its squad this year.

Each team has its own physiotherapists, masseurs, trainers, games analysts, trainers and rehabilitation workers. Some of these may be volunteers but the majority are paid employees of the club.

Both clubs have state of the art gymnasium and fitness facilities but soon City will have their new training facility costing around one hundred and sixty million dollars.

On a match day both clubs rely heavily upon its volunteers to assist their staffs to make sure everything runs smoothly. Without this army of volunteer workers both clubs would struggle to make their finances stretch to cover the necessary jobs that are required to be undertaken. The Adelaide Football Club can rely on up to 200 volunteers on match days to fill the various roles from selling raffle tickets to manning the car park gates.

Manchester City travel with a group of about 40 to each of their games. They will either travel by coach, rail or plane depending on where the game is being held. The Adelaide Crows, on the other hand, except for home games always travel by air. This is due to the logistics of getting around a country as large as Australia to visit the grounds in other states.

Both teams participate in competitions where team work is of the essence. The quick nimble footwork of the Manchester team against the high flying toughness of the Adelaide Crows show that the two games are very different in their styles but with both requiring extreme fitness and agility.

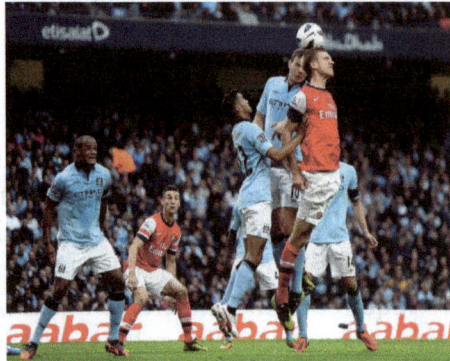

One code flies high with their head while the other leads with their hands. A spectacle, no matter what the code.

The Adelaide Crows, as it is with most Australian Rules teams rely very much on their supporters to act as volunteers on match days to man the various stalls, act as Stewards and

carry out many of the behind the scenes tasks. This highlights one of the vast differences between the two leagues as
every person working at Manchester City's home games is a
paid worker of the club.

The highlight of either team's week is the game which will be
over in less than two hours. A full week's work goes into
these two hours with players and coaching staff having ses-
sions most days. A big part of sport these days is the amount
of time being taken up with public appearances by the teams
either for television or radio commitments or attending functions to assist the many team sponsors. School coaching clinics and community events also require time to be provided
and the players, although well paid, spend many hours committed to the club other than being out on the field

HAVE YOU EVER WONDERED?

HOW A CITY'S TRAFFIC IS CONTROLLED?

To do this we visited the Traffic Management Centre that controls all traffic signs, signals and movements throughout South Australia. This centre is on a par with any other throughout the world. The main difference is that it is equipped to handle the traffic conditions in a state with a population of under two million people whereas other centres are designed to handle much larger volumes of traffic and some cities can have populations of in excess of 10 million people. Forgetting about the size of the centres they are all designed in similar fashion with an objective of the management of a particular areas traffic flow. One can only imagine the size of the centres in cities such as London, Tokyo, New York or Los Angeles where there can be up to 10,800 sets of traffic lights.

An inside view of the Traffic Management Centre showing the operator's consul where they will spend the first three months learning the different systems he will   control. Most major cities of the world have a centre such as this set up to guide the flow of traffic.

The South Australian centre always has a minimum of two operators at any one time and preferably three on day shift when the traffic can be at is heaviest. These operators when they begin their employment at the centre spend the first three months learning the systems   before being placed on the shift roster. Once here they will always have another more experienced operator guiding them. At present there are 13 operators working at the centre

Its operators work a 24/7 roster with always two on shift. The main system deployed at the centre is an Australian designed system known as SCATS. It controls all of the traffic lights throughout the state. . There are over 419 traffic light controlled intersections, 250 light controlled pedestrian crossings and 74 school crossings in South Australia with the number growing each year.   There is a strict criteria for installing a new set of traffic lights taking many factors into account. A new set of lights at an intersection can cost between eighty to one hundred and twenty thousand dollars with an ongoing cost of maintenance and power adding around another five thousand dollars each year. Approximately thirty light bulbs are replaced each day throughout the state and the centre is responsible for directing the maintenance crews promptly to each faulty light.

Information is fed into the centre by approximately 480 cameras, 140 of which are at road intersections. These cameras are usually mounted high over the roadway and can be adjusted to give a full 360 degree view. Throughout the roads of the state there are also electromagnetic loops embedded under the road surface. Most of these are at traffic light controlled areas. They are embedded under the road surface just prior to the white painted stop lines and can pick up on the metal in a vehicle stationary or passing over them. Each lane on the roadway has one of these loops and from it the system can determine the amount of waiting traffic at lights and the flow of traffic over the area. By determining the traffic density and flow the system will automatically adjust lights further along the road to cope. If a pad is faulty it will trigger an alarm back at the centre and a technician will be dispatched to rectify the problem. The consul operator can also view the intersection with the aid of the areas cameras and if he wishes to can observe the technician at work when he arrives. Not that there is much time in an operator's shift for doing this.

While the centre does not cover the rail traffic throughout the state their free call telephone number is displayed at all rail crossings and traffic signal boxes for members of the public to ring and report faults. This in turn allows the centre to communicate with the railway authorities to remedy faults on the rail system. They also take calls from members of the public wishing to report road hazards or unusual situations and will deal with these accordingly by either dispatching a road maintenance crew or notifying the relevant authorities of the matter.

The centre is also connected to the Government Radio Network allowing them to communicate direct with Police or the Fire Brigade. The centre controls the issue of permits for road works throughout the state and also the issue of permits for wide loads travelling throughout the state. The centre will adjust lights in these areas to cope with the road works or in the case of wide loads co-ordinate with the Police escorts to move the large cumbersome loads as fluently as possible through the built up areas.

One example of how the centre can assist with traffic flows is when a major football match is held at AAMI stadium. When football was first played at the West Lakes Stadium there was a requirement for sixteen policemen to be present to assist with the flow of traffic to and from the stadium. Now, by controlling the traffic lights in the surrounding area and also the dedicated bus lane from the centre they have been able to reduce the number of policemen to only four. This in itself is a major monetary saving to the authorities without taking into account the smoother flow of traffic.

By working the fire authorities the centre is able to facilitate a smooth run for the fire brigade as they attend fires. Every fire station has pre planned routes depending on the direction they are heading and these are programmed into the centres system that will be activated as soon as the fire personnel contact them as they are leaving the station. This system also works to assist the police Star Force on their routes to any situations they may have to attend as a matter of emergency.

The only emergency service that they cannot assist with is emergency calls to ambulances. Ambulances have what is referred to as a floating fleet. This means that they can be tasked from anywhere to attend an emergency with no way of pre planning desired routes. The fire service may be tasked between 50 to 80 times a day whereas the ambulance service can be anywhere between 300 to 1200 calls a day. To try and cope with this number of calls would crash any system of traffic management. There have been instances where the centre has been able to assist an ambulance in an emergency situation by co-ordinating the traffic signals on a particular route, but this is only in exceptional circumstances.

Besides the SCATS system the centre also operates another system referred to as STREAMS.

This system controls the electronic signage associated with freeways and also boom gates and traffic control signs. Both aforementioned systems work together well. On freeways there are detectors inserted under the road surface, one for each lane, with another set 500 metres further along. This allows the system to monitor the speed and flow of the traffic along the freeway and can also provide data as to the size of the vehicles. The first detector will provided data and if the next detector provides completely different data then the system will presume that something is happening on the road between them and warn an operator. The operator may then view camera images of the area to determine the cause.

With the section of the freeway that passes through tunnels fixed cameras are installed. These are able to detect unusually slow moving vehicle, pedestrians, stationary vehicles or fallen objects. They are currently being upgraded to show even a koala moving across the freeway.

The presently under construction South Road Freeway will be responsible for around another one hundred and sixteen cameras to manage the flow of traffic and assist in directing motorists by the use of co-ordination with overhead signalling.

The main aim of the Traffic Management Centre is to keep traffic flowing at an optimum. By doing this and being able to pin point major hazards they are able to reduce secondary incidents that may occur because of the original hazard. They have been able to reduce by twenty seven percent the number of secondary incidents happening on the roads today.

All digital video footage is kept for a period of six days and only released to the Police Department to assist in major incidents. Many a major crime has been solved with the use of footage from the centres network of cameras.

The only other footage that is kept is that which will be used for training purposes or may be used in television adverts by the Motor Accident Commission.

Car navigation systems such as Navman or Tom Tom gather information from the centre for use in their live traffic programmes.

The centre also controls the raising and lowering of the boom gates at each end of the Southern Expressway depending on the direction of traffic flow. By the use of their cameras they are able to ensure that the roadway is clear of traffic along its entire length before opening the boom gates.

The new road and rail bridges over the Port River are also under the control of the centre with them being able to open and close both bridges as required from their premises fifteen kilometres away. Infra-red cameras mounted in the vicinity show both road and river traffic in all types of weather conditions.

While the Adelaide centre is small by world standards the systems in use are of the equivalent standard to the larger cities. Centres of this type are utilised throughout the world with the one main objective.

Maintaining a safe steady flow of traffic though out its region.

The benefits to cities around the world with the same or similar systems in place are immeasurable.

1. They reduce road crashes.
2. They increase road safety with the early detection of signal faults and traffic problems.
3. They reduce vehicle emissions and fuel consumption.
4. They reduce traffic congestion.
5. They increase the traffic handling capacity of the roads.

Studies have shown that travel time can be cut by up to 20% and stops reduced by up to 40%. Couple these with a 12% decrease in fuel consumption and one can see that a systematic management of traffic is good for all.

HAVE YOU EVER WONDERED?

ABOUT THE PREPARATION REQUIRED BEFORE ONE OF THE WORLD'S GREAT JOURNEYS?

There are many great train journeys around the globe including the Trans-Siberian, The Royal Scotsman and the two Oriental Expresses. The train journey that we are going to touch on is, The Ghan, a rail trip from the bottom to the top of Australia, across the great Australian outback. It will carry you through a wilderness like no other. The Ghan first ran in the 1870's but at that time only went as far as Alice Springs and at that time the old steam engine took five days to make the trip and travelled at around forty kilometres per hour. It is a much faster trip these days with the line extended all the way to Darwin. The old trains had no mod cons such as air conditioning or refrigeration but the modern Ghan is almost like a five star hotel.

Each great train journey of the world has its own unique route covering countryside that might only be captured on that particular journey, and the Ghan is certainly one of these.

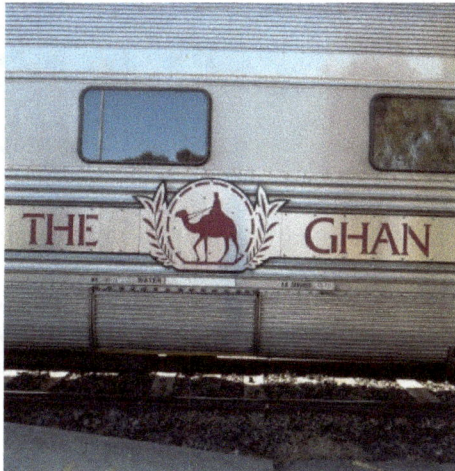

The Ghan's symbol is the camel and its handler, in recognition of the many Afghan cameleers and their journeys through the Red Centre. The journey itself is only twenty one kilometres short of three thousand and takes three days and two nights. On this trip you travel through the lush tropics of the Australian Top End across the red earth of Central Australia, through the magnificent Flinders Ranges to the south.

While each of the great journeys are different the preparation of the train for the trips are very similar even though they are spread across the globe.

The Ghan making one of its many river crossings.

There are longer or more lavish train trips available around the globe but the Ghan gives you a taste of everything. You have three levels of travel, from Platinum Class to Gold Class and lastly to Red Class.

The Queen Adelaide dining car and lounge car for Platinum and Gold Class passengers.

With new reservation options you are now able to lie in bed gazing at the passing scenery and take your breakfast at your leisure or stay longer over lunch to chat with new found friends. There is also the option of booking a table late at night for an intimate evening meal. Regional Australian cuisine is offered along the journey with all standard drinks, soft drinks and spirits included in your Platinum or Gold Service fare.

But what is the story in preparing this train for the journey.

Our chosen train, The Ghan, operated by Great Southern Rail, is staffed by a Train Manager; a Duty Manager; a Hospitality Manager and a Lounge Host. Sixteen Hospitality Attendants are supervised by the Housekeeping Supervisor and finally there are four Chefs to prepare all of the meals. All staff are house in basic shared facility carriages at the front and end of the train. The four train drivers also utilise the crew accommodation. In days gone by railways operated rest houses or barracks as they were then called and a train crew would rest up in one of those while a fresh crew took over the train. These days with crew accommodation travelling with the train there is no need to stop and change crews. There is the driver and his co-driver in the locomotive at any one time. They will swap positions every two to four hours and at the end of an eight hour shift the two new drivers will take over. Many liked the old system as they said they could get a better rest break and sleep if they were away from the train.

Staffing numbers are dependent on the number of carriages and the number of guests travelling aboard the train. Similarly fuel is dependent on how many carriages are connected to the power vans and how much power they draw, likewise the locomotives fuel use is dependent on how many locomotives are being used and how heavy or how many carriages they are pulling. Re-fuelling of our power vans and locomotives occurs in Adelaide, Alice Springs and Darwin. Usually there are two locomotives pulling the train which can stretch up to a kilometre in length and have a gross weight of around 1800 tonne. Each locomotive is capable of travelling either forwards or backwards at the same speed and the same amount of power being produced.

All of GSR's trains are serviced in Adelaide therefore the amount of train preparation is limited to time spent in Adelaide. For instance the Indian Pacific, a sister train to the Ghan, is only stationed at the Adelaide Parklands Terminal for approximately 3 hours, therefore servicing is done by experienced staff in a prompt manner. The carriages are run through a giant automatic wash which leaves them shining silver for the next trip. Within those three hours all food and beverages are loaded into their respective Queen Adelaide Restaurants and Outback Explorer Lounge cars. All fresh linen, towels and toiletries are loaded into each guest carriages as well as all guest carriages being serviced by our housekeeping staff. If any carriages are required for mechanical servicing they are taken off in Adelaide to be serviced, as well as additional carriages being needed to fulfil guests demands being added in Adelaide. Not only is the on-train preparation integral to the smooth operation of GSR's train but all of the support crew located throughout the country providing crucial support for when a train arrives at their station. Servicing of the locomotives however is a different matter. Once they were serviced according to the amount of mileage they had travelled, similar to the family car. Now they are serviced between 90 and 120 days with mileage not being taken into the equation. Oil quality is however monitored and the condition of it can depend if a locomotive is serviced earlier.

When the locomotive arrives at the service yard there will usually be two fitters and an electrician to carry out the service and a normal service can take as long as two eight hour shifts. Once all of the electrical components have been check and engine and brake checks finished the locomotive will be moved outside for refuelling of the diesel, water and sand tanks. The sand is carried in a tank connected by hoses to nozzles that are situated just in front and to the rear of the front and rear wheels of a bogey. This enables sand to be sprayed onto the metal line to give the wheels more traction in slippery conditions. Some locomotives carry up to twenty five thousand litres of diesel and can burn it up at the rate of one hundred litres every ten minutes.

Break downs or disruptions are generally out of GSR's control with a lot of other factors playing a role in small to large disruptions. GSR does not own or operate the locomotives that pull the rolling stock, this service is provided by Pacific National. If a locomotive breaks down we usually have two to nullify this issue and the second one can get the train out of trouble. Sometimes when only one locomotive is being used and it does fail another locomotive is sourced or there can be a long wait for it to be fixed. As majority of the track used for travel is single line if a train does happen to break down this can put delays all throughout the rail system. When these problems do occur all that can be done is to make sure the guests are comfortable and have all they need. There is the story of in the early days of the Ghan, the train breaking down in the middle of nowhere for nearly two weeks and the train driver having to go goat hunting to be able to feed the passengers.

One of the greatest memories that you will take away from on board one of GSR's train is that of your meals onboard. All of the fresh food deliveries are made to the train supplies in the days prior to the train departure and stored in a specific warehouse for sorting, quality control and loading onto the train. Ordering for an upcoming departure is done with the producers in the days leading up to a departure with updated guests numbers and requests. Specific ordering for guests with allergies and intolerances are done and special meals can be arranged prior to departure. Once the train arrives into the station the food is loaded onto the train into fresh/frozen and dry stock and then our on-board chefs pack the food into cupboards, fridges and freezers. All preparation work is done on board for all meals by the chefs, prepared fresh and served fresh.

The Ghan averages around eighty five to ninety kilometres per hour with a top speed of one hundred and fifteen. Of all the great train journeys of the world it is the longest on a north/south route and crosses an entire continent. Travelling at such a speed can be a problem with some of the animals that are encountered on a trip. There is the story of a train travelling at around 100 kilometres per hour and coming across six camels that were on a bridge over a large gorge. There was nowhere for the camels to go and the train certainly could not stop in time. It is said to be one of the messiest cleanups of any train pulling into Alice Springs.

When the train reaches its final destination it is all hands on deck as the train is cleaned from top to bottom and restocked with supplies for the return journey. A train is not making its owners a profit if it sits in a station for too long and turnaround times at each end of the journey are kept to a minimum.

HAVE YOU EVER WONDERED?

What the deadliest creature on the planet might be?

There are many differing ideas as to what the deadliest creature on the planet might be. Some may say the shark; others the crocodile or the snake. To help us decide we sought the help of an Australian person, Ben Cropp. Ben is a world renowned spear fisherman, underwater photographer and film maker and now conservationist. As such he has had extensive dealings with all of the above mentioned creatures and in his opinion they are all topped by the box jelly fish. . It is not only the most venomous jellyfish in Australia; it is the most poisonous animal in the world.

The most dangerous of them all is Australian Box Jellyfish (*Chironex fleckeri*) which is a big jellyfish, one of the biggest in Australia, and its venom is strong enough that it can kill many people in one go. Its stings have been described as the most painful burn the victims have ever experienced. The stings leave burning marks on the skin and the victim will lose consciousness rapidly and stop breathing

In Australia alone there have been over eighty deaths attributed to the Box Jelly Fish. This is the equivalent of the amount taken by crocodiles and many more than those killed by sharks. In Asia the figure would run into the hundreds. Much more is heard about the feats of the shark and crocodile but the box jelly fish takes away part of a lifestyle enjoyed by many. They breed in the tidal swamps and rivers around the coast line and around September to October make their way to the ocean and spread along the beaches. Stinger Season is the name given to the following months when it is most unsafe to swim in these waters. They were originally called Sea Wasps and are a jelly fish with remarkable senses. They can capture small fish and crustaceans quite easily with their trailing tentacles, paralysing them instantly. They are most intelligent and will avoid contact with humans if possible with most problems being encountered by swimmers blundering into them. The Jellyfish has extreme toxins present on its tentacles, which when in contact with a human, can stop cardio-respiratoryfunctions in as little as three minutes. They are pale blue and transparent in color and get their name from the cube-like shape of their bell. Up to 15 tentacles grow from each corner of the bell and can reach ten feet (three meters) in length. Each tentacle has about five thousand stinging cells, which are triggered not by touch but by the presence of a chemical on the outer layer of its prey and will inflict terrible pain and scarring, if you are lucky enough to survive a bad encounter. Females fare worse than men in encounters with these creatures because of their lack of hair over their bodies.

A large box jelly fish can measure around twenty five centimetres across its transparent bell and has an eye in each corner.

BOX JELLY FISH

They do however have predators with the two main ones being the hawk bill turtle and the blue swimmer crab.

The large box jelly fish only inhabits the first one hundred metres of water out from the coast line and when the water is calm will come right in almost to the shoreline. If the sea is rough they do not appear to like breaking waves and will stay out beyond the reach of them.

The second most dangerous jellyfish species in Australian waters is Irunandji (*Carukia barnesi*). It is a small jellyfish, only 12mm in diameter and it is transparent, so it's very hard to see. Like the Australian Box Jellyfish, Irukandji has got a box-shaped body, with one tentacle attached to each corner, which can be up to one metre long. Its sting is not painful and often not noticed, but the delayed effect about 30 minutes later includes nausea, vomiting, sweating and anxiety. Victims usually collapse with severe back-ache and muscle cramps. The majority of victims of these very small creatures need hospitalisation.

It is known to have killed two people in Australia but there may be more due to common misdiagnosis.

HAVE YOU EVER WONDERED?

How a female crocodile hunter achieved the feat of killing the world's largest salt water crocodile?

Until the white man came to Australia large salt water crocodiles had no enemy but themselves. The Australian Aboriginals who had inhabited the harsh and arid Australia for around forty thousand years hunted mainly the smaller crocodiles for food and collected the eggs. The large crocodiles were considered too hard to kill and left alone. With white settlement came cattle, horses, sheep, pigs and dogs all of which were to become prey to these large and voracious reptiles.

Crocodile hunting first came to the fore in the late 1800's but it was mainly carried out by stockman trying to protect the animals under their control. They were not professionals and the crocodile continued to plunder the waterways of northern Australia at will. They have been known in those early days to send many a lease holder to the wall by wiping out much of their stock.

It was not until the late 1940's that professional hunters came to the fore and many made a living by hunting and killing crocodiles. The crocodile skin was the main target and they would be sold to the skin buyers and then on into the fashion trade.

There were many crocodile hunters over the years but only three well known husband and wife teams. It is one of these teams, the most well known, that we will concentrate our story.

Ron and Krys Pawlowski came to Australia by quite differing means.

Krys spent much of her time in a Siberian labour camp when the Russians invaded her home of Poland. For three years she worked in extreme conditions of 50degree below zero at the camps. It was not until the temperature dropped below this figure that the detainees were not required to work. She eventually escaped and made her way across Siberia to the Persian border and to freedom. She later spent time in India and later in British East Africa near the foot of Mount Kilimanjaro. She eventually immigrated to Perth in 1950.

Ron, on the other hand escaped the Russians when they invaded Poland by first going into Czechoslovakia and making way to the American lines and freedom. He immigrated to Perth in 1949. He ventured into the mining industry and it was on one of his trips into Perth for supplies and to pick up mail that he met Krys. He had chosen a different boarding house to stay in than his usual as he had his dog with him and it turned out that Krys was the owner. They hit it off instantly and within a week were married. Within a month they had sold up all of their interests in Western Australia and packed three children, the dog and all of their possessions into a Holden sedan and headed off into the unknown.

Their trip took them to Karumba, a small town on the northern Australian coastline. There were only a few houses in the entire area but the area teemed with wildlife everywhere. They fell in love with the place and decided that this is where they would make their new home.

One day the children were playing outside when a three metre crocodile surfaced near them. Ron decided to kill the crocodile and eventually sold the skin. They received a cheque that was bigger than they expected and almost the equivalent on a man's weekly wage. They thought that this would be a way to make some money and so was borne the most famous husband and wife crocodile shooting team the country ever had. At first they had no idea what they were doing but were soon recognised as efficient hunters.

Ron decided to build a boat to assist with the new venture. This allowed them to venture   further from their home in the search for crocodiles. Soon a larger boat was required and a 22 foot fibreglass hulled boat with extra strengthening of the hull was in use. Now they could get to places that were only accessible from the sea and their extended trips proved quite profitable for them. Krys became something of a celebrity and wore jungle greens and bright red lipstick.

She went on to study to be a taxidermist and became an expert and set up a small business mounting crocodile hatchlings

At a press conference in Brisbane, Krys made a statement saying that although she spends hours wading knee deep through swamps in the search of crocodiles, it's good to catch a glimpse of her red nail polish as she pulls the trigger of the rifle.

Although Krys had never handled a firearm until she moved to Karumba she soon became a crack shot. It did not matter whether it was with a pistol or with a rifle shooting moving targets from a boat she was most efficient.

It was on a hot day in 1957 that Krys came across the monster croc that was to make her   famous. It was on the banks of the Normanton River and Krys dispatched the 8.63

metre crocodile with one shot just below the eye that killed instantly. She was to later say that she would never shoot one like that again. It was a magnificent creature. The two tonne creature was like no other that she had ever seen or would ever see again. Krys and Ron had seen this particular crocodile around for over a year and they had nicknamed it 'Pop' because they thought it was the grandfather of all crocodiles because of its enormous size. They had been cruising along one bank of the river, which at that time was about a quarter of a kilometre wide when Ron spotted 'Pop' on the opposite bank. He called out to Krys, who was down below making a cup of coffee and slowly made his way towards the other side of the river. Krys readied her .300 Magnum Winchester rifle and when they were within approximately 25 metres of the crocodile she shot it from the side through its ear, killing it instantly. The special bullets which they imported at a cost of five   shillings apiece make a small hole upon entry but fragment after that and would have scrambled the crocodile's brain instantly. They had decided to kill it as they did not want it to be riddled with bullets as other, not so experienced would most probably end up doing to eventually kill it.

"I was really sorry I shot him, poor fellow," she said. "He never woke up; he didn't know we were there. We couldn't move him, he was too big. "He was the most beautiful animal," Krys said.

This is the last know photo of Krys the Croc.

Ron and Krys estimated that they had killed approximately 10,000 crocodiles during their hunting career but that this was the one she most regretted. She described it as a beautiful animal. (a life size replica of Krys the Croc is on display in the main street of Normanton).

As a twist to this story, Ron and Krys, decided that enough was enough and began to deplore the killing of crocodiles and other wildlife. They started up an experimental crocodile farm and became two of Australia's earliest conservationists. Ron toured Australia and the United States trying to bring about the halting of the hunting of crocodiles and even addressed the United Nations re saving the crocodiles from extinction. He met firm resistance from the Queensland government and it went to ridiculous lengths to silence Ron. He never gave up, however, and in 1972 was invited to give evidence to the House of Representatives select committee on wildlife conservation. He stated that the crocodile population in Queensland had declined by around 98 percent since the

1950's and recommended a total ban on hunting of the animals. The Whitlam Labour government followed his advice and protected all salt water and freshwater crocodiles. The Queensland government was forced to follow suit.

The fearless crocodile hunter had now become its greatest protector.

'One Shot Krys' as she had been known passed away peacefully in 2004 and Ron remains alive to this day with his new wife just out of Cairns. A real gentleman, who led a life that we will never know again.

www.ingramcontent.com/pod-product-compliance
Lightning Source LLC
Chambersburg PA
CBHW072132020426
42334CB00018B/1768